Clinical Research at MENA

Fatih Özdener (ed.)

Clinical Research at MENA

Challenges and Solutions

PETER LANG

**Bibliographic Information published by the
Deutsche Nationalbibliothek**
The Deutsche Nationalbibliothek lists this publication in the Deutsche
Nationalbibliografie; detailed bibliographic data is available online at
http://dnb.d-nb.de.

Library of Congress Cataloging-in-Publication Data
A CIP catalog record for this book has been applied for at the
Library of Congress.

ISBN 978-3-631-81113-9 (Print)
E-ISBN 978-3-631-86385-5 (E-PDF)
E-ISBN 978-3-631-86386-2 (EPUB)
10.3726/b18862

© Peter Lang GmbH
Internationaler Verlag der Wissenschaften
Berlin 2022
All rights reserved.

Peter Lang – Berlin · Bern · Bruxelles · Istanbul · New York · Oxford · Warszawa · Wien

This publication has been peer reviewed.

www.peterlang.com

Table of Contents

List of Contributors

Ali Gokyer, MD
Medical Oncology, Trakya University, Medical School, Edirne, Turkey

Alihan Sürsal, MSc
Farmakon Research Development Training and Consultancy, Istanbul, Turkey

Aydın Erenmemişoğlu, MD
Professor of Pharmacology, Farmagen R&D Biot. Ltd, Gaziantep, Turkey

Barış Erdoğan, PhD
CEO, Clinerion Ltd, Basel, Switzerland

Bilge Aydın Temiz-LL.M
Vona Law Firm, Partner, Att.at Law & Mediator

Deniz Yüce, MD, PhD
Epidemiologist, Hacettepe University Cancer Institute, Ankara, Turkey

Fatih Özdener, MD, PhD
Associate Professor of Medical Pharmacology, Bahçeşehir University School of
Medicine, Istanbul, Turkey

Gökhan Özkan M.Sc.
Clinical Trials Department, Turkish Medicines and Medical Devices Agency,
Ankara, Turkey

Hamdi Akan, MD
Retired Professor of Hematology,
Head, Clinical Research Association, Turkey

İrfan Çiçin, MD
Professor of Medical Oncology, Trakya University, Medical School, Edirne, Turkey

Mehmet Yıldız
Assistant Professor of Pediatric Rheumatology, Istanbul University- Cerrahpasa,
Cerrahpasa Medical School, Istanbul, Turkey

Mutlu Hayran, MD, PhD
Professor of Epidemiology, Hacettepe University Cancer Institute, Ankara, Turkey

Nihan Burul Bozkurt, PhD
Head of Clinical Trials Department, Turkish Medicines and Medical Devices Agency, Ankara, Turkey

Ozgur Kasapcopur, MD
Professor of Pediatric Rheumatology, Istanbul University-Cerrahpasa, Cerrahpasa Medical School, Istanbul, Turkey

Peri Aytaç, Pharm. PhD
Novagenix Bioanalytical Drug R&D Center, Ankara, Turkey

Le Vin Chin
Head of Marketing & Communications, Clinerion Ltd, Basel, Switzerland

Zulfiye Gul, Pharm. PhD
Assistant Professor of Medical Pharmacology, Bahçeşehir University School of Medicine, Istanbul, Turkey

Fatih Özdener

General Picture of Clinical Research at MENA

Drug development processes are long and costly processes. The development of a drug can cost up to a billion dollars, and the whole process can take 10–15 years. The process of drug development involves in-silico and in-vitro trials, as well as animal testing. The most costly and long-lasting period of the development process is undoubtedly the clinical trials. Clinical trials often include phase studies ranging from a small group of healthy people to internationally organized multicenter trials on patients. In phase studies, the safety and the effectiveness of the drug are tested at every stage, starting with the healthy group and continuing with the patient group. Research products that successfully pass these phase studies begin to be prescribed by obtaining a license. Following the license obtainment, the safety of the drug continues to be monitored through safety notices during the routine postauthorization prescription.

The conductance of clinical trials is subject to a certain quality standard, called the Good Clinical Practices (GCP). Despite the application of these standards in the vast majority of countries where the clinical research is conducted, some countries are still in the adaptation phase with respect to these rules. The standard of quality ensures the quality of the most critical stages of clinical trials such as planning, execution, reporting, archiving, and most importantly, protecting the health and the well-being of the subjects participating in the clinical trial.

Historically, clinical studies have been conducted largely by the economically developed countries as a result of the aforementioned cost and time factors for the required studies, and the compulsory Good Clinical Practice standards. While there is an intense activity of clinical studies observed in some parts of the world, this activity is observably very low compared to the respective population in some other regions.

In this introductory section, the globally conducted clinical trials (CTs) are analyzed, and the number of these conducted clinical studies and their respective ratios to populations, types, and phases are evaluated. This evaluation was performed by scanning the ClinicalTrials.gov website in terms of the number of clinical studies performed in global regions, the number of pediatric CTs, the study type, the age group, the participation status of healthy volunteers, and the type of funding and fund providers. According to the results, it has been observed that most of the CTs have been conducted in North America and Europe (71 %), while the remaining minority (29 %) have been carried out in the rest of the world. The Middle East (ME) region, including Turkey, accounts for only the 4.5 % of all trials and ranks 4th after East Asia (11.5 %). The countries with the lowest number of CTs in the world include North Africa (1.6 %), other regions of Africa (1.5 %), and Central America (0.9 %) (Table 1 and Figure 1a).

Table 1: Distribution of CTs, CT phases, and pediatric CTs among the global regions

Region	Total CTs, (%)	Early Phase 1 CTs, (%)	Phase 1 CTs, (%)	Phase 2 CTs, (%)	Phase 3 CTs, (%)	Phase 4 CTs, (%)	Pediatric CTs, (%)	Population	CT Ratio ‰
Greenland	1 (<0.1)	0	0	0	0	0	1 (100.0)	56.8K	0.176
East, Central, West and South Africa	5587 (1.5)	17 (<0.1)	363 (6.5)	1024 (18.3)	1758 (31.5)	469 (8.4)	2456 (44.0)	1109.2M	0.101
North Africa	5629 (1.6)	77 (1.4)	215 (3.9)	701 (12.5)	853 (15.2)	614 (10.9)	1584 (28.1)	248.5M	0.227
Central America	3229 (0.9)	2 (0.1)	192 (6.0)	812 (25.2)	1472 (45.6)	212 (6.6)	1025 (31.74)	180.8M	0.179
East Asia	41,697 (11.5)	298 (0.7)	5244 (12.6)	7930 (19.0)	7366 (17.7)	4056 (9.7)	7170 (17.2)	1680.1M	0.248
Europe	103,914 (28.7)	386 (0.4)	9742 (9.4)	16,342 (15.7)	13,469 (13.0)	7577 (7.3)	17,139 (16.5)	747.9M	1.389
Middle East	16,189 (4.5)	90 (0.6)	871 (5.4)	2268 (14.0)	3210 (19.8)	1213 (7.5)	3901 (24.1)	291.8M	0.555
North America	153,375 (42.3)	2091 (1.4)	25,419 (16.6)	35,190 (22.9)	16,667 (10.9)	9707 (6.3)	30,850 (20.1)	371.1M	4.133
North Asia	6371 (1.8)	8 (0.1)	407 (6.4)	1622 (25.5)	3226 (50.6)	387 (6.1)	1091 (17.1)	108.7M	0.586
Pacifica	8396 (2.3)	20 (0.2)	1384 (16.5)	2185 (26.0)	3172 (37.8)	468 (5.6)	1547 (18.4)	41.6M	2.017
South America	11,393 (3.1)	40 (0.4)	481 (4.2)	1808 (15.9)	3555 (31.2)	1099 (9.7)	2371 (20.8)	432.5M	0.263
South Asia	5669 (1.6)	23 (0.4)	458 (8.1)	857 (15.1)	1626 (28.7)	512 (9.0)	1726 (30.5)	1951.4M	0.029
Southeast Asia	7366 (2.0)	24 (0.3)	664 (9.0)	1300 (17.7)	2116 (28.7)	680 (9.2)	1768 (24.0)	672.6M	0.110
World	365,282 (100.0)	45,433 (12.5)	3445 (1.0)	64,228 (17.7)	38,173 (10.5)	27,595 (7.6)	72,684 (20.1)	7836.7M	0.463

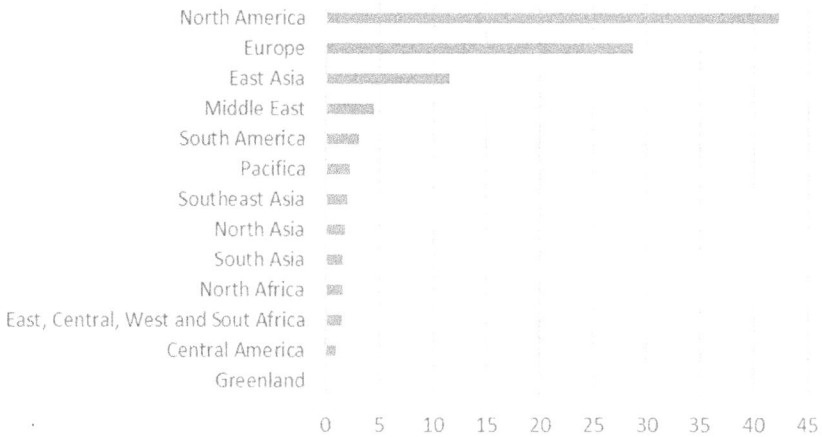

Figure 1a: Total CT percentages among regions

In terms of the number of CTs compared to the population, regions with the highest rate are North America, Pacifica, Europe, and North Asia. The calculation of this ratio for ME reveals that it is the region with the closest ratio to the world average. However, it is seen that both the world ratio and the ME ratio are still far behind as compared to regions where CTs are carried out with higher frequencies. For example, North America conducts approximately 8 times more CTs compared to ME, as seen in the respective percentages. The ratios of North Africa, which are very close to the ME region, show that the North African region is quite behind the world average, in that it is almost the half of the world average (Figure 1b).

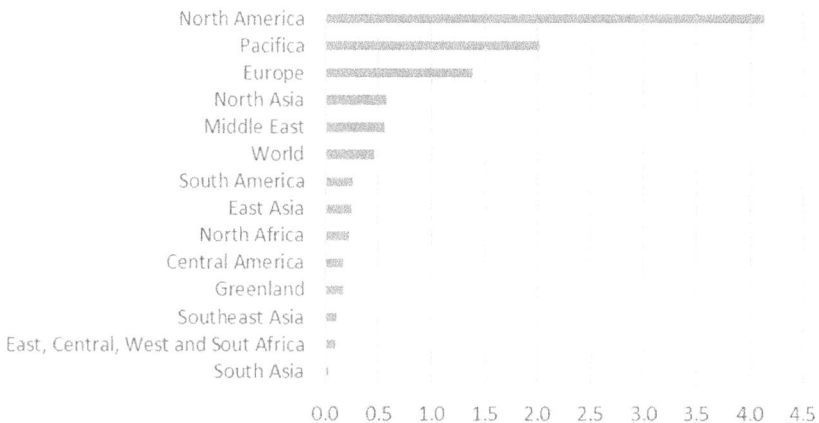

Figure 1b: CT to population ratio ‰

Figure 1c shows that phase 3 (late phase) studies are more common in other regions such as ME and North Africa, unlike North America, Europe, and East Asia where CTs are mostly conducted. However, it is observed that the number of phase 2 studies in North America, Europe, and East Asia, where clinical studies are conducted the most, is higher than the number of phase 3 studies.

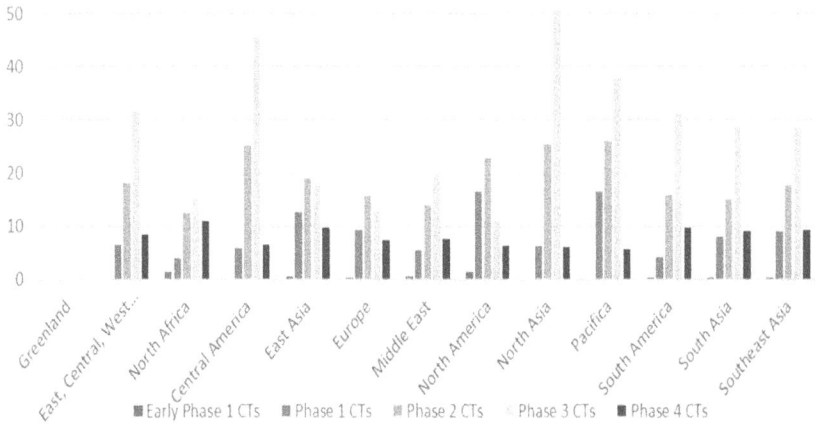

Figure 1c: Distribution of CT phases among global regions

The consideration of the target population for clinical studies in terms of age groups reveals an interesting statistic, suggesting that pediatric studies are relatively low in regions such as North America, Europe, and East Asia where many clinical studies are conducted. Accordingly, the clinical study ratios with this population are not very high in these regions. It is interesting to note that while the pediatric population ratios in ME are generally stable and at a moderate level, the ratios of clinical studies with this population are higher in North Africa despite the low number of general clinical studies (Figure 1d).

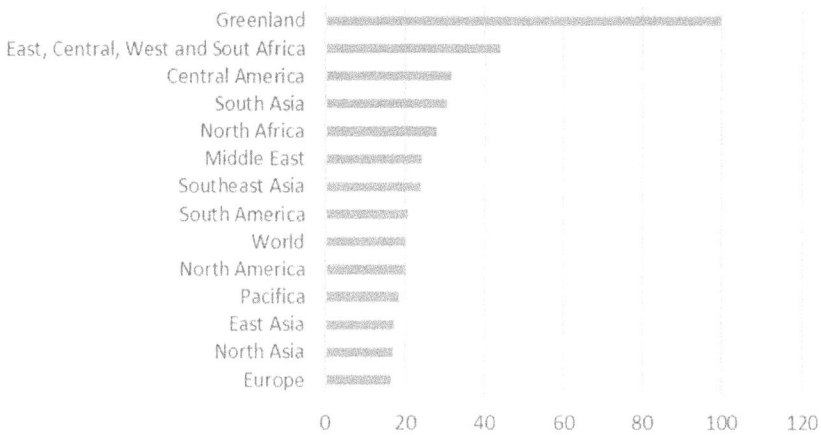

Figure 1d: Ratio of pediatric CTs to the global

Through the examination of the ME region, which is the homeland of the authors of this book, in more detail by taking the global position of the region in clinical studies as a reference, it is suggested that the following factors stand out in the ME region compared to the global statistics (Table 2 and Figure 2).

A. It is seen that less interventional studies and expanded access program studies are carried out.

B. It is seen that more observational studies and patient registry studies are conducted.

C. It is also seen that more pediatric group studies and fewer adult and older adult population studies are carried out.

D. It is observed that healthy volunteers take part in the studies at the same rate as the global average.

E. It appears that there are more industry-sponsored studies involved.

Table 2: The number of different types of CTs and their percentage in ratio to the global

	Number of CTs in ME	Number of CTs in the Global	ME ratio to the global (%)
Study Type			
Interventional Studies	12,277	284,495	4.32
Observational Studies	4025	78,203	5.15
Patient registries	544	7102	7.66
Expanded Access Studies	28	719	3.89
Age Group			
Child (birth-17) Studies	3933	72,997	5.39
Adult (18–64) Studies	14,715	336,249	4.38
Older Adult (65+) Studies	11,383	278,249	4.09
Healthy Volunteers			
Studies including healthy volunteers	3986	92,245	4.32
Studies excluding healthy volunteers	12,344	272,029	4.54
Funding			
Industry Funded Studies	5556	115,814	4.80
Studies Funded by Other Funds	10,800	251,331	4.30

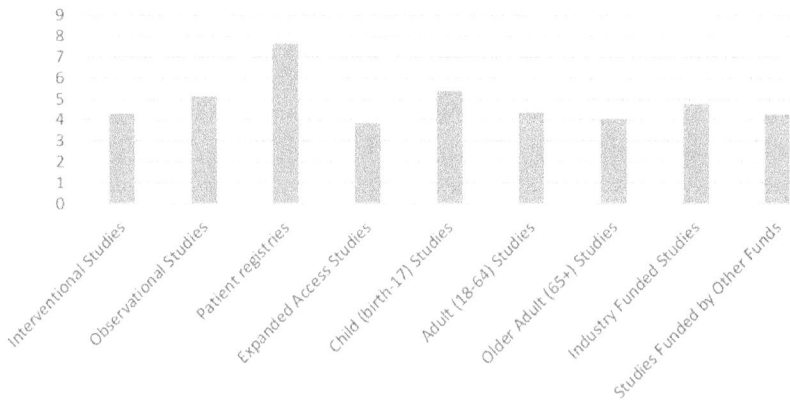

Figure 2: The number of different types of CTs in ratio to the global

The comparison of different countries in the ME region according to their respective population sizes reveals that the country where the most number of clinical studies is conducted is Israel (8.936). Other countries that are above the world average (0.463) are Cyprus (1.370), Lebanon, (0.810), Turkey (0.747), and Qatar (0.505). The ratio of clinical studies to the respective population is below the world average for other countries (Table 3 and Figure 3).

In conclusion, the MENA region offers significant opportunities for clinical research. The realization of these opportunities will depend on correct identification of the barriers and high degree of cooperation between different stakeholders to remove them.

Table 3: Distribution of CTs among countries of ME and their ratio to ME

ME Countries With Highest CTs	Number of CTs	Ratio of CTs to ME
Israel	8042	49.25
Turkey	6125	37.51
Iran	1083	6.63
Saudi Arabia	823	5.04
Lebanon	555	3.40
Jordan	285	1.75
United Arab Emirates	265	1.62
Qatar	143	0.88
Cyprus	120	0.73
Kuwait	119	0.73

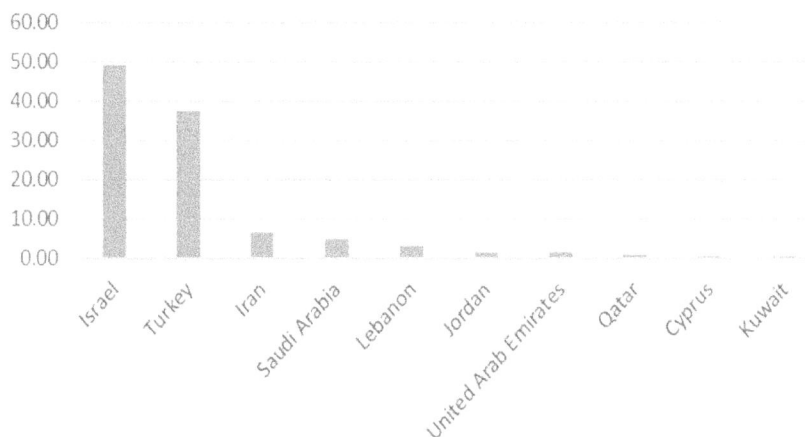

Figure 3: Ratio of CTs among countries of ME to total number of CTs conducted in ME

References

1. Kunal S. Ultimate Guide To Clinical Trial Costs 2017 [cited 2019 April]. Available from: https://clinicaltrialpodcast.com/ultimate-guide-to-clinical-trial-costs/.

2. Aronson JK. What is a clinical trial? British Journal of Clinical Pharmacology. 2004;58(1):1–3.

3. Friedman LM, Furberg C, DeMets DL, Reboussin DM, Granger CB. Fundamentals of clinical trials. Springer, 2010.

4. Molzon J, Giaquinto A, Lindstrom L, Tominaga T, Ward M, Doerr P, et al. The value and benefits of the international conference on harmonisation to drug regulatory authorities: Advancing harmonization for better public health. Clinical Pharmacology & Therapeutics. 2011;89(4):503–12.

5. Drain PK, Parker RA, Robine M, Holmes KK. Global migration of clinical research during the era of trial registration. PLOS ONE. 2018;13(2):e0192413.

6. Nair SC, Ibrahim H, Celentano DD. Clinical trials in the Middle East and North Africa (MENA) Region: Grandstanding or grandeur? Contemp Clin Trials. 2013;36(2):704–10.

7. National Library of Medicine. ClinicalTrials.gov 2019, February 27. Available from: https://clinicaltrials.gov/ct2/home.

Hamdi Akan

Clinical Trial Designs of the Future – Getting Ready at MENA

For many years, clinical trials on investigational new drugs (INDs) are conducted in a well-established pattern. Starting from Phase I studies, the INDs are tested in Phase II and Phase III trials and are continued as Phase IV studies after the authority approval. At the end of each phase, the study is terminated and data collected from the study are analyzed and reported. If the results are deemed satisfactory, the next phase is initiated.

This process is repeated at each phase until the IND receives authority approval. Although this is a well-established system, it is a time consuming, labor-intensive, and a costly process.

There are several problems with this traditional approach:

1. The time required to develop a new drug is around 9–12 years.
2. The cost of developing a new drug is more than 1 billion dollars.
3. New emerging diseases such as EBOLA, SARS, and COVID-19 need a rapid drug or vaccine development.
4. Orphan diseases are extremely rare, and clinical trials frequently cannot enroll a sufficient number of patients.

There are two basic approaches to overcome these problems:

A. Speeding the Regulatory overview
B. Using new design and methods

The COVID-19 pandemic revealed the need for other alternatives to develop new vaccines and drugs and test the old drugs against emerging diseases. This problem was encountered during the high-fatality EBOLA epidemics, and adaptive trial design was employed to expedite the trial process and develop a vaccine during an outbreak (1, 2).

The remainder of this review will address these two topics and attempt to discuss how MENA countries can cope with this problem.

Speeding the Regulatory Overview

The review of a clinical trial protocol and other documents is a hard task that requires considerable time and expertise. Although there are well-established timetables, the process takes a long time due to queries and revisions during this period. Accelerating this process can be beneficial, particularly in the case of emerging diseases awaiting new treatments. In order to overcome this problem, FDA developed several pathways such as (3):

- **Accelerated Approval is for a drug candidate intended for critical conditions and may provide a significant advantage over available therapy. It makes use of a surrogate endpoint.**
- **Priority Review is designed for a severe condition, and the trials have resulted in a significant improvement. The review period has been reduced from ten to six months.**
- **Fast Track is for a drug candidate designed to treat a serious condition, and that demonstrated in non-clinical studies the potential to address an unmet medical need.**
- **Breakthrough Therapy designation is for a drug candidate intended to treat a critical ailment and has preliminary clinical evidence indicating that it may be a substantial improvement over available therapy.**

These are called "FDA expedited review," and all of these programs are aimed at serious and life-threatening diseases. These reviews sometimes require a lengthy process and direct contact with FDA. From 2011 through 2018, FDA approved 200 out of 367 novel drugs (54 %) that utilized at least one expedited development tool (4).

As in Turkey, many countries develop similar procedures like Fast Track. Although the effectiveness of these alternative review approaches has been demonstrated, it remains limited (5).

MENA Countries

One of the main problems in the Middle East and North Africa (MENA) region is the absence of specified regulations for the review process. While certain countries, such as Turkey, with a parallel track review process (concomitant ethical committee and authority submission) benefit from this opportunity and have an authority approval period of fewer than eight weeks, this may be longer in other countries with a sequential submission process. There may be several ways to improve this process such as:

A. having definite timelines for the EC approval process.
B. having a fast-track possibility for life threatening and emerging diseases.

Another critical point to make is the need for training and educating clinical researchers and ethics committee members in every aspect of clinical trials to ensure that they have a clear understanding of the admission and submission processes.

Using New Design and Methods

The discovery of a new drug is time-consuming, very costly, and demands a high level of organization and near-perfection in quality control. When the entire process is considered, it is clear that most of the time, budget, and effort is spent during the clinical trial period (6).

According to a study conducted by TUFTS University in the United States of America, the cost of developing a new drug, including failures, was 2.5 million USD in 2014 (7). The failures are a big problem. Paul et al. reported success rates of 51 % for discovery research, 69 % for preclinical development, 12.8 % for the clinical development phases and 91 % for the submission phase, resulting in an overall probability of technical and regulatory success (PTRS) for drug R&D of 4.1 % (8). Another analysis showed that only 9.6 % of the investigational new drugs that entered Phase I had the chance to get authority approval in 2018 (9).

While these constraints increase the cost of drugs on the market, they also disappoint the society awaiting for new therapies for emerging diseases and health problems such as obesity, Alzheimer's, and so on.

In order to overcome this problem, there is an ongoing search for novel approaches that can shorten clinical trial phases while simultaneously helping for more economical use of clinical trial participants.

The initial attempts started in the 1980s with the introduction of **group sequential design**. The main idea behind this approach is to terminate the clinical trial early in the event of significant success, failure, or futility. This may result in a clinical study being completed considerably more quickly, with fewer participants than initially planned, and eliminating the risks of unnecessarily exposing clinical trial participants to the adverse reactions associated with INDs in the event of failure or futility. In a group sequential design, early termination rules are specified prior to the clinical trial, and then the interim analysis is conducted by an Independent Data Monitoring Committee (IDMC). The board considers the termination rules and may determine whether or not the IND was significantly successful or failed. In the event of success or failure, the trial may be terminated prematurely, avoiding excessive resource consumption and further exposing patients to the adverse reactions associated with the INDs.

This is also true if the Institut National pour la Recherche Biomedicale (INRB) determines that there is no need to continue the trial as it will not be able to prove the concept (futility).

This design was first introduced in a Cardiology study with success (10), and other studies followed this path. Over the last decade it has been clear that this approach may be beneficial not only for terminating a clinical trial early but also for continuing the trial and making certain adjustments based on the interim analysis results. These trials are named as **Group Sequential Adaptive Trials**. Adaptive trials became a valuable tool, and authorities published various documents to implement this approach to the drug development process to reduce the duration of the clinical trial as well as prevent some problems that may result in bias (11). Adaptive clinical trial designs gained popularity during this time period.

Adaptive Clinical Trial Design

This term denotes that during a clinical trial, several aspects of the trial can be modified using the data of the interim analysis performed by the IDMC. Usually, the timing of the interim analysis, the structure of the IDMC, the data that will be used during the interim analysis (recruitment rates, primary and secondary endpoints, safety, patients leaving the trial early, data quality, etc.) and whether the analysis will be masked or open are defined before the start of the trial. Additionally, the adaptations (modifications) have to be decided and submitted to the Ethical Committees before the trial (sample size, number of arms, randomization, inclusion and exclusion criteria, etc.)

In countries taking part in hematology and oncology trials, it will be quite common to participate in clinical trials with new design terminologies such as Umbrella, Basket, and Seamless trials. Since they are not classical clinical trials, it is necessary to become familiar with the terminology. In Basket trials, the trial begins with a group of cancers that share common targets and are tested with new drugs; the failing cancer set is taken out of the trial, and the trial continues with the winners. In Umbrella trials, cancer with different mutations is included, and different drugs targeting these different mutations are used. The failing drug/s are taken out of the trial, and the trial continues with the winners. Seamless trials are trials with two different consecutive phases that continue uninterruptedly based on the interim analysis of the independent review committee. Additionally, there are other approaches, such as trials with a biomarker endpoint rather than a clinical outcome, adaptive enrichment, and so on (11, 12).

MENA Countries

The ethical committees and regulatory authorities are used to review clinical studies with a classical overflow in terms of phases. In a classical clinical trial, first Phase I is conducted, analyzed and if successful followed by Phase II and then Phase III. Adaptive trails are different than this approach. You can easily switch to a second Phase (Phase I to Phase II, Phase II to Phase III) without terminating and analyzing one phase. This will save a lot of time, effort and may end with fewer number of patients in a trial, thus will be cost-effective. This approach is sometimes misunderstood by ethical committees, and the committees may require the results of the previous phase before starting the consecutive phase. As two phases may operate seamlessly, this can cause an unnecessary delay and require added communication with the regulatory bodies and ethical committees. For this reason, the regulatory bodies and ethical committees should:

A. be ready for the submission of trials with adaptive design, especially in the era of COVID-19 pandemic.
B. provide opportunities to contact, inform and advice the sponsors and investigators during the conduct and review of the clinical trial.
C. have more emphasis on the Independent Data Review Committees.
D. provide education and information on adaptive trials, especially to the ethical committee members.
E. seek the help of external reviewers for adaptive trials when needed.

COVID Pandemic

There are three main pathways to have clinical trials on COVID-19 in a MENA country; being a part of a global COVID-19 clinical trial or developing your own vaccine or drug or to use old drugs for COVID-19 in a national/international clinical trial. Nowadays in Turkey there are 13 COVID-10 vaccine trials that are going on and three of these trials are local vaccine trials. The number of clinical trials on COVID-19 are increasing rapidly and in MENA countries, to be a player in both pathways is a good opportunity to overcome the negative public opinion on clinical trials, as people are more eager to be a part of COVID-19 clinical trials.

Especially the efforts to develop new vaccines and drugs against COVID-19 brings out the need for new measures and exemptions. Both FDA, EMA and joint bodies such as International coalition of medicines regulatory authorities (ICMRA) published guidelines to facilitate the development of novel strategies against COVID-19 (13). These guidelines cover both preclinical and clinical phases of developing a novel drug or vaccine. An example of such an exemption is stated in the ICMRA Global Regulatory Workshop on COVID-19 Vaccine Development as: "Some vaccine constructs for which there is adequate support from the knowledge around the immune response elicited may be allowed to proceed to FIH (First in Human) trials without first completing animal studies to assess the potential for enhanced disease provided adequate risk mitigation strategies are put in place in these FIH trials." Adopting such strategies and having a fast track option for COVID-19 studies will be a good initiative to bring new studies on COVID-19 to a MENA country.

Digital Transformation and Clinical Trials

While digital transformation is shaping the new world, it also had a great impact on clinical trials – in all phases such as planning, submitting, reviewing, conducting and publishing a clinical trial. Especially artificial intelligence is going to be a major part of conducting and data processing in a clinical trial. Also the advantages of using new technologies and devices to monitor the patient and data opened a new phase in clinical trials. Pharmaceutical companies and Clinical Research Organizations (CROs) are talking about this subject more and more in the past few years. While the focus is more on virtual remote monitorization, remote tracking of drug use and accountability, and remote informed consent obtaining triggered by COVID-19 pandemic, there are also a lot of work on using artificial intelligence in different parts of a clinical trial (14).

MENA Countries

The introduction of remote management in clinical trials will also help to maintain the integrity of a clinical trial without patient loss, problems in obtaining informed consent, missing visits, missing monitorizations, undelivered drugs and data loss. For MENA countries with a good Internet backbone and IT capacity, these will a positive incentive to bring more clinical trials to a MENA country.

References

1. PREVAIL II Writing Group; Multi-National PREVAIL II Study Team; Davey RT Jr, Dodd L, et al. A Randomized, Controlled Trial of ZMapp for Ebola Virus Infection. NEJM. 2016 Oct 13;375(15):1448–1456.
2. Dodd LE, Proschan MA, et al. Design of a Randomized Controlled Trial for Ebola Virus Disease Medical Countermeasures: PREVAIL II, the Ebola MCM Study. J Infect Dis 2016 June 15;213(12):1906–13.

3. https://www.fda.gov/patients/learn-about-drug-and-device-approvals/fast-track-breakthrough-therapy-accelerated-approval-priority-review. Accessed on 12 October 2020.

4. https://www.fda.gov/news-events/fda-voices/delivering-promising-new-medicines-without-sacrificing-safety-and-efficacy. Accessed on 12 October 2020.

5. Timeline of various approval tracks and research phases in the US. Graph credit: Kernsters – Graph created based on information provided in Scientific American article, "Faster Evaluation of Vital Drugs", CC BY-SA 3.0, https://en.wikipedia.org/w/index.php?curid=39972696

6. Prasad V, Mailankody S. Research and Development Spending to Bring a Single Cancer Drug to Market and Revenues After Approval. JAMA Intern Med. 2017;177(11):1569–1575.

7. Tufts Center for the Study of Drug Development briefing. 18 November 2014. https://www.youtube.com/watch?v=EcGJm5FrMPA. Accessed on 11 October 2020.

8. Paul SM, et al. How to Improve R&D Productivity: The Pharmaceutical Industry's Grand Challenge. Nat Rev Drug Discov. 2010;9:203–214.

9. Mullard A. Parsing Clinical Success Rates. Nat Rev Drug Discov. 2016;15:447. https://doi.org/10.1038/nrd.2016.136.

10. Beta Blocker Heart Attack Trial. https://biolincc.nhlbi.nih.gov/studies/bhat/. Accessed on 12 October 2020.

11. Adaptive Design Clinical Trials for Drugs and Biologics Guidance for Industry. December 2019. https://www.fda.gov/regulatory-information/search-fda-guidance-documents/adaptive-design-clinical-trials-drugs-and-biologics-guidance-industry. Accessed on 14 October 2020.

12. Pallmann P, Bedding AW, Choodari-Oskooei B, et al. Adaptive Designs in Clinical Trials: Why Use Them, and How to Run and Report Them. BMC Med. 2018;16:29. https://doi.org/10.1186/s12916-018-1017-7

13. Development and Licensure of Vaccines to Prevent COVID-19 – Guidance for Industry. ICMRA June 2020.

14. Harrer S, Shah P, Antony B, Hu J. Artificial Intelligence for Clinical Trial Design. Special Issue: Rise of Machines in Medicine. Trends in Pharmacological Sciences. August 2019;40(8):577-592. https://doi.org/10.1016/j.tips.2019.05.005

Nihan Burul Bozkurt, Gökhan Özkan

The Role of Regulatory Authorities and TITCK

The lengthy, costly, and multi-component venture of pharmaceutical research and development (R&D) offers exciting possibilities as it ultimately aims to promote human health. The adventure of a pharmaceutical product starts with discovery and continues through preclinical and clinical studies. This process ends when the candidate drug is licensed upon meeting the efficacy and safety requirements. After that, it is ready to promote human health. The clinical trials account for the lengthiest and most expensive component of the pharmaceutical R&D adventure. The cost of this 10–15-year process can reach up to 2.5 billion US dollars. Throughout this process, the candidate molecules that are deemed eligible in terms of efficacy and safety in preclinical studies are tested in clinical trials. Innovative drugs are usually expected to successfully complete Phase I, II, and III clinical trials before they can be licensed. Only one out of thousands of drug candidate molecules completes the R&D adventure successfully, and only 9.6 out of 100 drug candidates entering Phase I studies are licensed. The total costs of Phase I, II, and III studies account for 50.2 % of the total cost for the R&D of a drug. The R&D stages that innovative drugs go through are shown in Figure 1 (1–4).

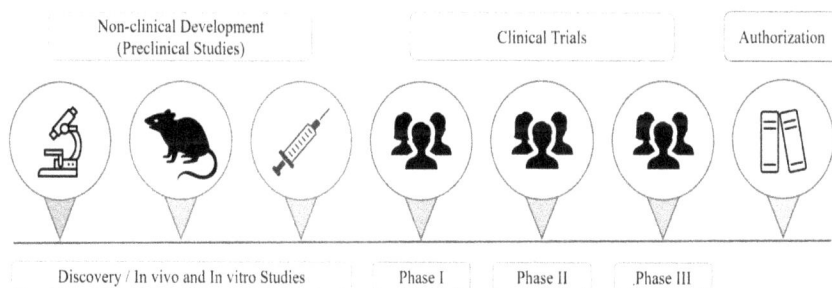

| Non-clinical Development (Preclinical Studies) | | | Clinical Trials | | | Authorization |

| Discovery / In vivo and In vitro Studies | Phase I | Phase II | Phase III |

Figure 1: The innovative pharmaceutical R&D process

The safety and effectiveness of medical devices, diagnostic/therapeutic products, and methods must be proven, as well as the drug candidate molecules, through a series of scientific studies in order to become available for general public use. Clinical trials are defined as prospective studies conducted on humans for the purpose of investigating the effects of one or more health-related interventions on human health outcomes (health, behavior, body structure, and functioning of humans) by The World Health Organization (WHO). The intervention in this definition refers to any interventional product, activity, or process including pharmaceuticals, medical and biological products, herbal products, medical devices, surgical methods, and dietary strategies (5).

In order for medicines and medical devices to be made available to the public, they must be manufactured at certain quality standards, and their effectiveness and safety must be ensured. The efficacy and safety of such products are extensively evaluated during clinical trial stage, which is the most critical step in the R&D process. Clinical trials have long become the best and most strictly regulated field in the world due to extensive regulations. These strict regulatory rules are applied in order to protect the rights and safety of volunteers, and to ensure data quality. The authorities that regulate and supervise the pharmaceutical and medical device industries are among the most influential agencies in the world since these fields keep humans in the center of their activities and are in direct contact with public health.

The major function of regulatory authorities is to develop national regulations in line with internationally accepted ethical principles, international conventions, and valid scientific information. The purpose of these regulations is to meet the current needs and transparency concerns of the studies so as to assess respective clinical trial applications accordingly. A well-regulated clinical trial environment instills confidence in sponsors, clinical trial teams, clinical trial sites, volunteers, and, ultimately, the whole society. Consequently, establishing mutual trust across clinical trial parties is one of the most important parameters for achieving improvements in the clinical trial field.

Clinical Trial Motivations and Regulatory Authorities

Sponsors take various criteria into account when selecting countries where clinical trials will be conducted. The most important criteria for country selection can be listed as follows:

1. Volunteer potential and volunteer recruitment rates
2. Availability of experienced study sites and investigators
3. Access potential to volunteers from various races and with different types of diseases,

4. Predictable and competitive costs
5. Clinical trial incentives
6. Permission processes and the regulatory environment
7. Harmonization with global clinical trial trends

The first five items depend mainly on the clinical trial environment and the infrastructure of individual countries. The reasons for selecting a country for conducting clinical trials include treatment options that are easy to access, favorable disease incidences, competitive clinical trial costs, availability of volunteer pools, improved healthcare provision, qualified investigators, well-equipped centers, specialized clinical study sites, and R&D incentives.

The last two criteria depend mostly on the extent of the development of the regulatory environment, harmonization with international regulations, and competencies of regulatory authorities. Factors that put countries ahead with respect to the "regulatory environment" in question include the ease of the clinical trial application processes, predictable and short periods to obtain permission, the structural integrity of regulations, transparency, and the attitudes of regulatory authorities toward new trends and developments.

It is crucial for the authorities to provide supervision, and to actively fulfill the regulation and inspection functions. In order to improve the clinical trial ecosystem, it may be useful for regulatory authorities to execute activities under different categories in cooperation with relevant stakeholders. The consequences of such activities would reflect on the ecosystem favorably.

Clinical Trial Authorities and Clinical Trial Regulations in Turkey

The first independent organization to regulate the field of clinical trials in Turkey is the "General Directorate of Pharmacy and Medicinal Products," established in 1946. The organization was renamed the "General Directorate of Pharmaceuticals and Pharmacy" in 1982. Later, the Legislative Decree No. 663 on the Organization and Duties of the Ministry of Health and its Affiliates, published in the Official Gazette No. 28103 dated 02.11.2011, transformed the General Directorate into an agency called the Turkish Medicines and Medical Devices Agency (TITCK) affiliated to the Ministry of Health, with an allocated special budget. Since that specified date, the field of clinical trials has been essentially organized by the TITCK (6).

After the implementation of the Presidential Government System, Presidential Decree number 4 published in the Official Gazette, dated 15.07.2018 with issue number 30479, described the duties of the Agency. Accordingly, the Agency is responsible for putting regulations into effect, and performs inspections in parallel to the policies and objectives of the Ministry of Health, concerning the following goods: medicines, active substances and excipients used in drug production, substances subject to national and international control, medical devices, in vitro diagnostic devices, traditional herbal medicinal products, cosmetic products, homeopathic medicinal products, biocidal products in direct contact to the human body, and special-purpose diet food (7).

According to Presidential Decree number 4, developing regulations, issuing authorizations, and performing inspections within the scope of duty in the field of clinical trials on medicines, medical devices, and products are included in the duties of TITCK (7).

The history of clinical trial regulations in Turkey is deep-rooted. There are many legal regulations and sub-regulations that exist in this field. Concerning the participation in clinical trials, the following essentials have long been included in the country's legislation including obtaining consent from the individual, complying with scientific and ethical principles in planning and conducting clinical trials, and the requirement to obtain authorization from the regulatory authority following the approval of the ethics committee.

Article 17 of the Constitution of the Republic of Turkey issued in 1982 states that the protection of the corporeal integrity of the individual is one of the most important personal rights, and that a person shall not be subjected to scientific or medical experiments without his/her consent. Thus, it is clearly stated that clinical trials cannot be performed on individuals without his/her consent. The requirement to obtain consent from respective individuals is a constitutional obligation to protect the rights of the individuals (8).

Article 70 of the law on the Practice of Medicine and Medical Arts dated 11 April 1928, issued with the number 1219 stipulated that clinical trials cannot be conducted without obtaining the consent of the individual, and that if a clinical trial is planned to be carried out on minors or incapacitated and legally prohibited persons, the consent of the parents or guardians should be additionally obtained (9).

The k-clause of the third article of the Fundamental Act on Health Services No. 3359 dated 7 May 1987 prohibits the use of drugs and their preparations in humans for scientific research purposes unless the permissions from the Ministry of Health and the consent of the person are obtained. Regarding the requirements for conducting clinical trials, the additional 10th article of the same law put a broad-framed regulation into effect in 2011 (10).

Article 90 of the Turkish Criminal Code No. 5237 dated 26.09.2004 describes the constitutional conditions and the respective penal sanctions concerning the crime of "experimentations on humans" (11).

The "Convention for the Protection of Human Rights and Dignity of the Human Being with regard to the Application of Biology and Medicine: Convention on Human Rights and Biomedicine," which was prepared in accordance with the recommendation of the Council of Europe Parliamentary Assembly on the preparation of a bioethics convention, was opened for signature on 4 April 1997 in the Council of Europe. In Turkey, this Convention was accepted by Law No. 5013 on 3 December 2003 by the Grand National Assembly of Turkey. The Biomedicine Convention entered into force after it was published in the Official Gazette dated 20 April 2004 and numbered 25439 (12).

As can be seen from the legislative regulations mentioned above, it can be stated that Turkey has one of the best regulatory systems in the field of clinical trials based on the grounds of being a party to international conventions and having the national legislation regulating the field over many years. Concerning the regulatory authority, the existence, awareness, and inclusiveness of the regulations favorably serve the clinical trial environment in the country.

An examination of sub-regulations reveals that the first regulation on clinical trials in Turkey was published in 1993. Changes were made to this regulation in the years 2008, 2010, and 2011, depending on the needs over time. The regulation on Clinical Trials of Medicinal and Biological Products, which is currently in effect, was published in 2013. In 2014 and 2015, various articles of the regulation were updated. This regulation standardized clinical trials of medicines, medicinal and biological products, and herbal products, including bioavailability and bioequivalence studies, to be carried out on humans even when such a product is licensed or granted permission for use. The Regulation has been prepared in parallel with the Directives 2001/20/EC and 2005/28/EC of the European Union's legislation on good clinical practices on medicinal products for human use (13).

Twenty-two guidelines have been published in order to implement the regulation and guide the clinical trial parties. These guidelines are listed in Table 1. Guidelines that provide comprehensive guidance on many issues such as the algorithm to be followed in clinical trial applications, obligations for safety reporting, requirements for clinical trial liability insurance, import of investigational medicinal products, investigator meetings, and clinical study training programs have been published over time, and continue to be published by the Agency (14).

Table 1: Current clinical trial guidelines in Turkey

Guideline for Good Clinical Practice
Guideline for Observational Drug Studies
Guideline for Clinical Trial Applications Made to the Clinical Trials Department of the Turkish Pharmaceuticals and Medical Devices Agency
Guideline for Clinical Trial Applications Made to Ethics Committees
Guideline on Ethical Approaches in Clinical Trials Conducted in the Pediatric Population
Guideline for Principles and Standards for Good Clinical Practice Applications of Advanced Therapy Products
Guideline on Biological Materials Management in Clinical Trials
Guideline for Clinical Trial Liability Insurance
Guideline for Safety Reporting in Clinical Trials
Guideline for Development Safety Update Report for Clinical Trials
Guideline for Applications for Clinical Trial Investigator Meetings
Guideline for Planning and Assessment Principles for Clinical Trial Training
Guideline on Site Organization Management Principles in Clinical Trials
Guideline on Independent Data Monitoring Committees
Principles of Standard Operating Procedures for Ethics Committees of Clinical Trials and Bioavailability-Bioequivalence Studies
Guideline on the Structure and Working Procedures and Principles of the Bioethics Board
Principles of Standard Operating Procedures for the Clinical Trial Advisory Board
Guideline on the Storage and Distribution of Investigational Medicinal Products Used in Clinical Trials
Guideline for Archiving Principles in Clinical Trials
Guideline for the Import of Investigational Medicinal Products to Be Used in Clinical Trials
Guideline on Nonclinical Evaluation of Vaccines for Human Use
Guideline on Nonclinical Evaluation of Animal Immunoglobulin/Immune Serums Against Viral and Bacterial Agents for Human Use

Turkey has been following the "E6 Good Clinical Practice (GCP)" guideline published by the International Council for Harmonization of Technical Requirements for Pharmaceuticals for Human Use (ICH) since 1995. Turkey has adopted and implemented the guideline by making the necessary adjustments according to internal policies (15).

The legislation environment in Turkey is harmonized with the regulations of the European Union and ICH, and has been adjusted to growing new trends in the world. The consistency and functionality of the Turkish legislation with international standards provide advantages for the clinical trial environment in Turkey.

There are several developments that necessitate adaptations via legislative adjustments due to the changes in application and documentation processes in clinical trials. These developments include the increasing use of adaptive clinical trial design protocols and different varieties of clinical trial designs such as basket or umbrella designs, advances in the use of real-life data, the increasing importance of patient reported outcomes, digital solutions becoming a significant component of clinical trials, and the increasing complexity of investigational medicinal products.

The shortcomings and harmonization issues about the above-mentioned subject matters in the clinical trial legislation constitute a group of challenges facing the authorities. Regulations need to be updated in the continuously evolving clinical trial environment in order to make the necessary adjustments in line with new developments. In this context, having national authorities, who can readily adapt to developments in the field and can guide the parties involved in the conductance of clinical trials, offer opportunities for countries.

Clinical Trial Application Processes

The components that are of most importance among the many factors (e.g. cost, planning, sustainability) in the clinical trial field are the easiness, understandability, and the predictability of the application processes. In addition to these factors, rapid assessment and authorization processes put countries ahead in the global race in the clinical trial field as well.

In this sense, two steps are very important in facilitating the clinical trial application process and making it understandable. These are the provision of information/transparency regarding the application processes and the implementation of online application systems.

For example, the year 2014-EU Clinical Trial Regulation, which is still in transition, introduced a new process regulating that a single clinical trial application package submitted through a common portal would be valid for all member countries so that countries could make a joint decision on a certain timetable. Moreover, rigid decisions were made through the introduction of the "silent agreement" concept concerning the length of the assessment of clinical trial applications. The objective of the regulation is summarized in terms of establishing consistent rules to be valid in all EU countries, and ensuring the transparency of the approval, conduct, and publication processes of the clinical trial results (16).

By the year 2016, studies had come out concerning the development of the infrastructure of the clinical trial information systems and the facilitation of the clinical trial application processes. In 2018, TITCK launched the web-based "Clinical Trials Module" for online submissions in order to standardize clinical trial applications, ensure efficiency in time management, and build up an effective database. Furthermore, the clinical trial application guidelines were updated, and the entire application process became more clear and standardized. Through this update, all aspects of clinical trial applications including how the applications should be submitted, which documents will be submitted, and the assessment times have been specified and published transparently (17).

The Module has provided significant convenience in data management through the inspection and supervision of TITCK on clinical trials. Moreover, the Module could serve as a resource for the licensing, inspection, and pharmacovigilance functions of TITCK.

Clinical trial data on medicinal products and medical devices have been published on the "Clinical Trials Portal" (*kap.titck.gov.tr*), which is a local database of Turkey, since 2014. Thanks to the established integration between the Portal and the Module through improvement efforts, the most up-to-date information about the clinical trials in Turkey has been made available comprehensively. The new version of the portal provides instant up-to-date information such as the volunteer recruitment status, clinical study sites, investigational products, and clinical study types. Furthermore, the system allows users to run a keyword search as well (18).

The development studies of the Clinical Trial Module and the Clinical Trial Portal continue at a fast pace. Development studies continue to make more functional decision support systems for the module by setting up alert systems for applicants, improving the search function of the portal, publishing summary study results for laypersons, and publishing more information in general.

Hence, end-to-end data management and transparency have been achieved through the existing structure of the systems. Through the created database, TITCK provides various types of clinical trial information to both applicants and the public.

Major advances have been recorded in the assessment of clinical trial applications through the implementation of a successful process management procedure. Thus, the duration for the first assessment of a clinical trial application decreased to 26 days in 2019, while it averaged to 100 days in 2016. According to the regulations in Turkey, the time that should be spent for the assessment of a clinical trial application was specified as 30 days. The analysis of the data collected in 2020 revealed that assessments were completed within the 30 days of the submission for 98.93 % of the clinical trial applications. In parallel to all these improvements, the number of new clinical trial applications in Turkey rose to 477 in 2020, while this figure was 391 in 2012. In the last three years, an increase of 12 % has been achieved in the number of actively conducted clinical studies.

Harmonization with International Regulations

Some clinical trials may be conducted in multiple countries due to the international nature of clinical trials. The conductance of such studies in more than one country with a similar and/or equivalent regulatory environment increases trust in the obtained clinical data. In this respect, it becomes a necessity to have common international guidelines and principles to be followed by countries. Memberships/partnerships to international business associations/consortiums by countries and country representatives provide the grounds to be preferred by global companies for conducting clinical trials in those countries.

Aiming to standardize the regulatory activities for drug development, the International Council for Harmonization (ICH) has become operational in 1990 upon the joint decision of the pharmaceutical authorities of the USA, the European Union, and Japan along with some pharmaceutical industry representatives as founding members. ICH mainly develops standardized guidelines to ensure the fulfillment of quality, efficacy, and safety requirements in the fields of licensing of drugs, clinical trials, and pharmacovigilance. ICH regularly updates these guidelines in line with scientific and technological developments. After the implementation of several structural reforms in the constitution of ICH, regulatory authorities other than the founding and permanent members were also admitted to membership (19–21). TITCK was admitted to ICH as an observer member on 7 June 2018, and as a full member on 27 May 2020. The admission has substantiated that clinical trial activities in Turkey conform to the international standards. Upon the ICH membership, Turkey was included in the expert group for the revision of the International Conference on Harmonization-Good Clinical Practices (ICH-GCP) guideline, which has been accepted as the international standard in the field of clinical trials (22, 23).

International Pharmaceutical Regulators Programme (IPRP) became operational in 2018 by the consolidation of the International Pharmaceutical Regulators Forum (IPRF) and the International Generic Drug Regulators Programme (IGDRP) (24). The objective of IPRP is to provide an environment for the exchange of information across members and observer members, enable cooperation, and promote harmonization of regulatory approaches for pharmaceutical medicinal products for human use (25). After the admission to ICH as an observing member, TITCK has been invited to IPRP and became a member of the organization. IPRP is an organization in which the health authorities of the member countries are the members. IPRP aims to enable cooperation across the member authorities, foster the evaluation of current issues, promote information exchange on common interests, and ensure convergence in the regulatory field for pharmaceutical drugs for human use.

Upon the participation of member countries of the European Free Trade Association in 1971, the Pharmaceutical Inspection Convention (PIC) was founded. In order to pave the way for different drug authorities to become members of the convention, the Pharmaceutical Inspection Convention Scheme (PIC/S) was founded in 1995 to operate in the field of international adaptation and improvements of the Good Manufacturing Practice (GMP) inspection standards (26). In 2013, TITCK applied to become a full member of PIC/S. On 1 January 2018, TITCK was admitted to the PIC/S membership (27).

These memberships and cooperations are indicators that Turkey closely follows and implements the international standards for clinical trials. In addition, memberships to international organizations provide an entry to international platforms guiding new regulations and standards, and help catch up with global trends and be informed of developments at an early stage.

Convergence with Global Trends and Actions Taken in Response to New Developments

The more proactive the regulatory authorities are toward new trends and developments, the sooner clinical trial parties can adapt their organizational arrangements to the new requirements. This saves time for clinical trial parties and provides authorities the opportunity to set out the rules and deliver guidance. Countries that are ready and able to adapt quickly to new developments in the clinical trial environment are more attractive for clinical trial parties as well.

The most recent example in this regard is the actions taken and the regulations made by authorities for clinical trial executions under the pandemic conditions during the COVID-19 outbreak. During the pandemic, while it has been necessary to reduce the burden conferred by the COVID-19 pandemic on the existing clinical trials, it has also been necessary to promote the conduct of clinical trials about vaccines and COVID-19 treatments in the fastest way possible.

On 19 March 2020, TITCK published a document called *Measures to Be Taken in Clinical Trials Due to the COVID-19 Pandemic* immediately after the announcement of the first case in Turkey. It was followed by another document about the frequently asked questions regarding clinical trial processes during the pandemic. Thus, the implementation of necessary precautions was enabled early in the pandemic, and the operations and procedures to be carried out by all parties involved in clinical trials were organized beforehand to minimize personal contact as much as possible (28–30).

Along with the global efforts, Turkey prioritized clinical trials on COVID-19 vaccines and new treatment options. During this process, a fast track assessment process for COVID-19 studies has been implemented by TITCK.

TITCK closely followed all scientific advances about the development of COVID-19 vaccines, and carried out guiding activities for groups developing vaccines in parallel to international studies. Acting proactively, TITCK has developed the "*Table of Requirements for Viral Vaccine Candidates for Transition to Clinical Trials*," which contains detailed information to guide parties that plan to conduct clinical trials about COVID-19 vaccines. This document was effectively communicated to all stakeholders (31, 32). In the meantime, TITCK provided guidance to all parties involved in vaccine development studies by publishing the "*Guideline on Nonclinical Evaluation of Vaccines for Human Use*" about the studies required to be completed before the transition to the clinical trial phases. In that guideline, exceptions were specified to be put into effect in "Emergency Public Health" situations, which were, and still, valid for the current pandemic conditions (33).

The effect of the measures taken was evaluated by collecting feedback from companies involved in the conduct of clinical trials. In these feedbacks, all companies reported that TITCK swiftly published the respective measures to be taken. In addition, it was reported that 90 % of the companies found the measures very useful, and 10 % found them useful in helping create action plans in order to meet the urgent needs (34). During the pandemic, the number of clinical trials fell with respect to the previous year in the US, where the highest number of clinical trials are conducted in the world. However, the number of clinical trials increased in Turkey in the year 2020 as compared to the previous year (35).

Clinical Trials in the MENA Region

An analysis of the number of all clinical trials registered on the "clinicaltrials.gov" web page by the end of 2020 reveals that 66.80 % of clinical trials in the world were conducted in America and Europe. Meanwhile, the clinical trials conducted by countries in the MENA[1] region account for only 4.76 % of the

---

1   Based on MENA countries registered at the worldbank.org web page.

studies conducted in the world. Moreover, the consideration of only the number of clinical trials registered on the "clinicaltrials.gov" web page in 2020 shows that 52.35 % of the clinical trials were from America and Europe, while 5.92 % were from the MENA region. Proportionally, the share of MENA countries from globally executed clinical trials is quite low (35).

In response to the higher number of clinical trials in the US and other European countries, pharmaceutical companies have been driven to conduct clinical trials in other countries due to the increasing clinical trial costs in the US and European countries, the increasing workload on clinical trial sites, and the pharmaceutical industry's search for new drug markets. Hence, the conduct of clinical trials in the MENA region has gained an increasing momentum in recent years in the presence of these challenges and opportunities to increase the share from global clinical trials.

The number of clinical trials executed in the US and Europe is high as a natural consequence of the fact that the vast majority of pharmaceutical R&D activities take place in these regions. In order to become more efficient in terms of clinical trials and R&D activities, developing countries should analyze the pharmaceutical R&D ecosystem as a whole, and improve and reinforce this ecosystem in all aspects. Furthermore, in order to attract clinical trials conducted by global companies, developing countries should adopt a competitive mindset as they are competing with countries with an established clinical trial infrastructure and health system, as well as sufficient manpower. Each step taken in the following areas including the ease of clinical trial processes, times required to obtain permissions, consistency, transparency, predictability, international collaborations, patient databases, patient recruitment rates, data quality, and low costs will create an environment of opportunity for these countries.

Challenges faced by regulatory authorities in MENA countries may include the lack of sufficient and experienced manpower, inadequacy and inexperience in the field of information technologies, incompatibility across countries in the conduct of clinical trial processes, language barriers, and deficits in transparency and communication. However, the most significant challenge can be listed as the lack of standardization across ethical committees to perform ethical and scientific assessments of clinical trials. The comparability of assessment processes and durations facilitates predictability. In this context, the deviations from the predicted timelines and the different assessments across ethics committees put developing countries in unfavorable positions.

The analysis of the number of registered clinical trials on the "clinicaltrials.gov" web page reveals that while the number of clinical trials conducted in the MENA region was 17.243, the number of clinical trials conducted only in Turkey was 6.041. Turkey is the second country after Israel in conducting most of the clinical trials in the MENA region (35). In fact, clinical trial operations of many companies in MENA countries are managed from Turkey. In this sense, Turkey is a model country in the MENA region with respect to the achievements in the field of clinical trials over the recent years, as well as its position between the developed countries and the MENA countries, and the well-established clinical trial experience. In parallel to national policies, Turkey continues its efforts and initiatives with determination in line with its goal of becoming a regional leader in clinical trials.

References

1. Hughes JP, Rees S, Kalindjian SB, Philpott KL. Principles of early drug discovery. British Journal of Pharmacology 2011;162 (6):1239–1249.

2. DiMasi JA, Grabowski HG, Hansen RW. Innovation in the pharmaceutical industry: new estimates of R&D costs. J Health Econ. 2016;47:20–33.

3. PhRMA. Biopharmaceutical Research Industry Profile 2016.

4. Clinical Development Success Rates 2006–2015 – BIO, Biomedtracker, Amplion 2016.

5. World Health Organization, International Clinical Trials Registry Platform (ICTRP). Access date: 01.12.2020. Retrieved from https://www.who.int/clinical-trials-registry-platform

6. Turkish Medicines and Medical Devices Agency, History. Access date: 01.12.2020. Retrieved from https://www.titck.gov.tr/kurumsal/tarihce

7. Presidential Decree No. 4 on the Organization of Affiliated, Related, and Associated Institutions and Organizations to the Ministries and Other Institutions and Organizations (2018), TR Official Gazette, issue: 30479, date:15.07.2018.

8. Constitution of Republic of Turkey (1982), TR Official Gazette, issue: 17863, date: 11.09.1982.

9. Law No. 1219 on the Practice of Medicine and Medical Arts (1928), TR Official Gazette, issue: 863, date:14.04.1928.

10. Health Services Fundamental Law No. 3359 (1987), TR Official Gazette, issue: 19461, date: 15.05.1987.

11. Turkish Penal Code No. 5237 (2004), TR Official Gazette, issue: 25611, date: 12.10.2004.

12. The Convention for the Protection of Human Rights and Dignity of the Human Being with Regard to the Application of Biology and Medicine: Convention on Human Rights and Biomedicine No. 5013: The

Law on the Approval of the Convention on Human Rights and Biomedicine (2003), TR Official Gazette, issue: 25311, date: 09.12.2003.

13. Regulation on Clinical Trials of Medicinal and Biological Products (2013), TR Official Gazette, issue no: 28617, date: 13.04.2013.

14 Turkish Medicines and Medical Devices Agency, Clinical Trials. Access date: 15.12.2020. Retrieved from https://www.titck.gov.tr/faaliyetalanlari/ilac/klinik-arastirmalar

15. Turkish Medicines and Medical Devices Agency, Legislation. Access date: 01.02.2021. Retrieved from https://www.titck.gov.tr/mevzuat/2150

16. European Medicines Agency, Clinical Trial Regulation. Access date: 15.12.2020. Retrieved from https://www.ema.europa.eu/en/human-regulatory/research-development/clinical-trials/clinical-trial-regulation

17. Turkish Medicines and Medical Devices Agency, Announcements. Access date: 18.12.2020. Retrieved from https://www.titck.gov.tr/duyuru/3640

18. Turkish Medicines and Medical Devices Agency, Clinical Trials Portal. Access date: 18.12.2020. Retrieved from https://kap.titck.gov.tr/

19. ICH About ICH / History. Access date: 08.11.2020. Retrieved from https://www.ich.org/page/history

20. ICH, ICH Increases Its Global Reach, Moves Forward on Global Drug Development. 2016.

21. Lindström-Gommers L, Mullin T. International Conference on Harmonization: Recent Reforms as a Driver of Global Regulatory Harmonization and Innovation in Medical Products. Clin Pharmacol Ther. 2019 Apr;105(4):926–931. doi: 10.1002/cpt.1289.

22. Turkish Medicines and Medical Devices Agency, News. Access date: 15.01.2021. Retrieved from https://www.titck.gov.tr/haber/1234

23. Turkish Medicines and Medical Devices Agency, News. Access date: 15.01.2021. Retrieved from https://www.titck.gov.tr/haber/1392

24. IPRP History. Access date: 15.01.2021. Retrieved from http://www.iprp.global/page/history

25. IPRP Mission. Access date: 18.12.2020. Retrieved from http://www.iprp.global/page/mission

26. PIC / S History of PIC / S. Access date: 01.02.2021. Retrieved from https://picscheme.org/en/history

27. Turkish Medicines and Medical Devices Agency, News. Access date: 15.01.2021. Retrieved from https://www.titck.gov.tr/haber/1392

28. Turkish Medicines and Medical Devices Agency, Announcements. Access date: 10.02.2021. Retrieved from https://www.titck.gov.tr/duyuru/3755

29. Turkish Medicines and Medical Devices Agency, Announcements. Access date: 10.02.2021. Retrieved from https://www.titck.gov.tr/duyuru/3801

30. Turkish Medicines and Medical Devices Agency, Announcements. Access date: 10.02.2021. Retrieved from https://www.titck.gov.tr/duyuru/3755

31. Turkish Medicines and Medical Devices Agency, Announcements. Access date: 18.02.2021. Retrieved from https://www.titck.gov.tr/duyuru/3892

32. Turkish Medicines and Medical Devices Agency, Legislation. Access date: 10.02.2021. Retrieved from https://www.titck.gov.tr/duyuru/3801

33. Turkish Medicines and Medical Devices Agency, Legislation. Access date: 01.02.2021. Retrieved from https://www.titck.gov.tr/mevzuat/2150

34. Association of Research-Based Pharmaceutical Companies (AIFD) Survey dated 17 August 2020.

35. US National Library of Medicine Clinical Studies Registry and Results Database. Access date: 15.01.2021. Retrieved from https://clinicaltrials.gov/

İrfan Çiçin, Ali Gökyer

Role of Investigator

Introduction and Definitions

With a population of about 600,000, the MENA region constitutes about 7 % of the world population. With an annual population growth of 1.7 %, the population of the region increases above the world average (1, 2). Although its population is close to that of the European continent, the number of clinical studies conducted in the MENA region is about one-fifth of that of Europe (1, 3). On the other hand, regulations on clinical studies have been introduced in several MENA countries since the beginning of 2000. However, no significant increase has been observed in the number of clinical studies in these countries except for Turkey and Egypt (4–6). Health authority and regulations, institutions and their managerial approaches, researcher potential and their attitudes, and the socio-cultural and economic structure of the society are significant factors in the development of clinical research (3–6) (Figure 1). With their high education levels, international relations skills, and entrepreneurial-transformative approaches, the researchers, who constitute one of the major components of these factors, can contribute significantly to the development of clinical studies in countries.

CLINICAL RESEARCH
ENVIRONMENT AND
DEVELOPMENT

HEALTH AUTHORITY ATTITUDE
AND REGULATIONS

MANAGERIAL ATTITUDES OF
RESEARCH CENTERS

RESEARCH POTENTIAL AND
ATTITUDES

SOCIAL PERSPECTIVE

Figure 1: Clinical research environment components

The U.S. Food and Drug Administration (FDA) defines the researcher as a person responsible for conducting a study in a center. If the study is carried out by a team in a center, a researcher becomes responsible for the team, and the responsible researcher is called as "principal investigator" (7). Other researchers in the clinical studies are called as "sub-investigators." On the other hand, the "assistant researcher" is the other researcher delegated by the principal investigator, who generally plays a critical role in conducting the study. If the clinical study is a multicenter study, the role of the principal investigator is to manage the study process at the center. However, if it is a single-center study, the principal investigator is entirely responsible for conducting the study. On the other hand, the definition and responsibilities of the researcher may change according to the source of funds for the research. If the principal investigator is only responsible for conducting the study in his/her own center in a multicenter study funded and designed by industry or other institutions, he/she is called "center researcher." In cases where the responsibility of the design and other processes of the study is taken by the researcher and the fund is obtained from any source, he/she is called "sponsor researcher" (8, 9). The latter concept refers to the studies initiated by the researcher (Figure 2).

Researcher:
Person responsible for conducting the study in a center

Principle Investigator
Researcher responsible for conducting the study in the research team

Assistant Researcher
Researcher taking part in the study under the supervision of the principal Investigator in a study team

Center Researcher
Principal Investigator in a multicenter research

Sponsor Researcher
The researcher who has the general responsibility of conducting studies when it is initiated by the researcher

Figure 2: 'Researcher/Investigator' definitions

As can be seen from the definitions above, the duties and responsibilities of the researcher may vary depending on the roles undertaken. Therefore, the problems encountered and the solution proposals may vary according to each role. Since the assistant researcher is responsible for performing the tasks delegated by the principal investigator, in this section, the term "researcher" will be used to describe the principal investigator, and all findings and solution proposals will be stated accordingly. The concept of "sponsor researcher" will be discussed separately to highlight its different aspects.

Multicenter Industry-Sponsored and Academic Clinical Trials

Problems and Solutions

The question of where the researcher's responsibility begins and where it ends is the least known or described issue in terms of researchers, researchers' institutions, local regulations, and perhaps national regulations. Knowing and describing a clinical research process in detail is the best way to reveal the researcher's role and responsibilities, problems, and solutions.

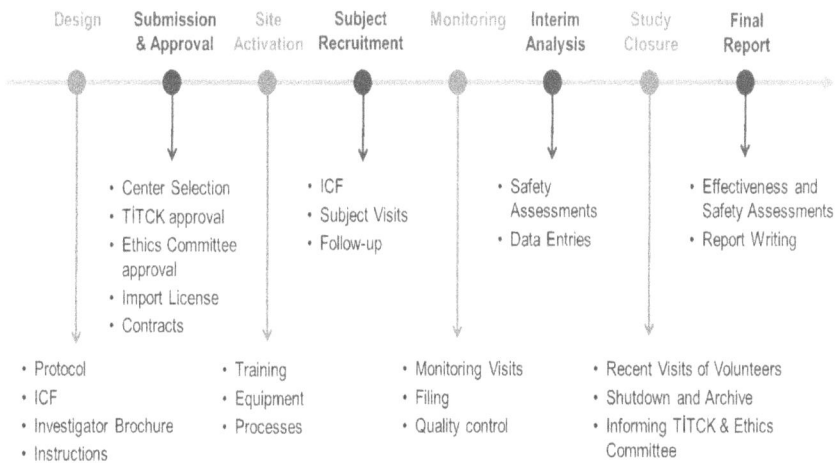

Figure 3: Clinical research processes (10)

In the clinical trial processes given above, center researchers can directly affect the processes shown in bold (Figure 3). Center researchers do not involve or have any responsibility in the processes of preparing the study protocol, Informed Consent Form (ICF), investigator brochure, and the instructions at the beginning of the research apart from those initiated by the researcher. They only contribute to these processes afterward by providing feedback. After completing these processes, the most critical stage in a clinical trial is the selection of the center/researcher. The basic expectation of the sponsors of a clinical trial is to achieve high-quality and accurate results at the expected time (Figure 4, 5) (11, 12). At this point, while the researcher is responsible for conducting the study with the expected efficiency in the center, the researcher's institution, that is, the management process of the center, is responsible for establishing the infrastructure to ensure carrying out the study under ideal conditions. One of the major problems of the researchers in the clinical trial environments with insufficient readiness is that they have to provide consultancy for regulations and infrastructure in their centers. After determining the candidate center /researcher for the interest of clinical trial, the sponsors submit their applications to the national authorities and ethics committees. Then, they begin the procedures of other processes of the clinical trials based on the permissions they receive. Therefore, the first stage of achieving a clinical trial is regarded/known as the candidate.

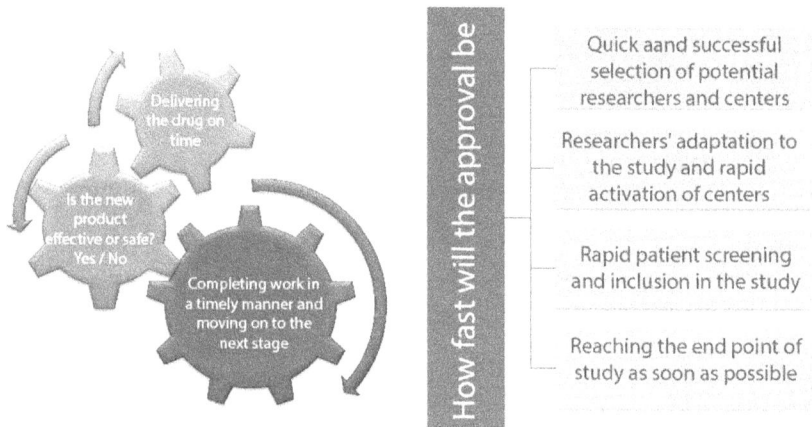

Figure 4: Clinical trials are expected to provide fast, accurate, and auditable information

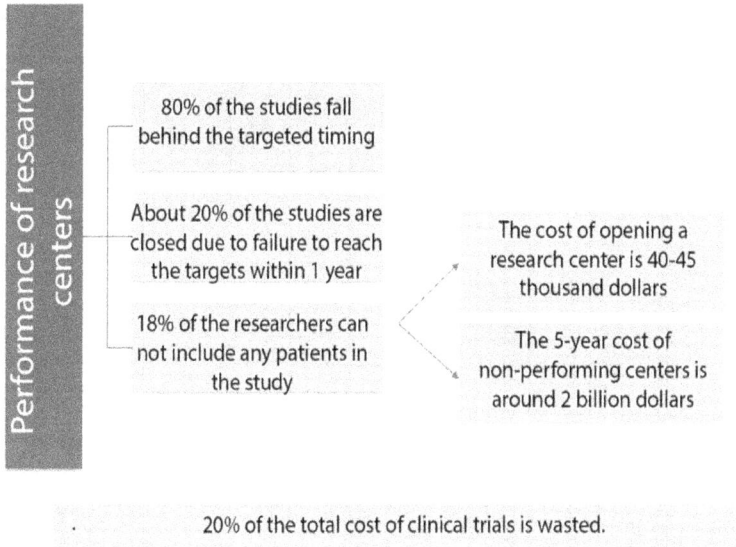

Figure 5: Inefficiency of clinical research centers causes significant economic and time losses

Center Selection
Problems

Establishing clinical trial units or centers with an unsystematic organization based on the initiative of the researcher or several institutions rather than establishing the infrastructure of the clinical trials using a national network is one of the most critical problems (5, 10, 13–16) (Figure 6). Therefore, a small number of permanent and well-known centers could be established by the personal efforts of researchers. Researchers who are willing to research but do not have the opportunity to be visible due to environmental conditions and several other reasons cannot access the clinical trials. Table 1 shows the problems that can be classified into two groups regarding the selection of center/researcher.

Table 1: Research center features created with the initiative of the researcher

	Permanent and Known Centers Created with Researcher Initiative	Permanent and Unknown Centers Created with Researcher Initiative
1	Usually, in big cities and institutions.	Relatively small cities and provinces.
2	Close contact with research environments already due to their localization.	Contact with research environments may be weaker.
3	Institutional infrastructure possibilities may be more.	The researcher may need to prepare the institutional infrastructure.
4	The institutional administrative structure is more ready.	Institutional administrative structure may need to be adapted to the work.
5	It is easier to provide experienced, trained staff in the clinical study team.	It may be difficult to find experienced trained personnel for the clinical study team.
6	In-house working partners may cause problems in conducting the study.	Same situation.
7	Researchers being envied of academic and economic gains by their colleagues.	Same situation.
8	Approaches that break the standards can be seen around the question of whether the owner of the study is the researcher or the center.	Same situation.
9	Numerous studies increase the burden of the researcher and the center, and quality can be affected.	The number and variety of patients may be low. Due to participation in studies that are not compatible with the center's potential, poor performance negatively affects subsequent center selection processes.

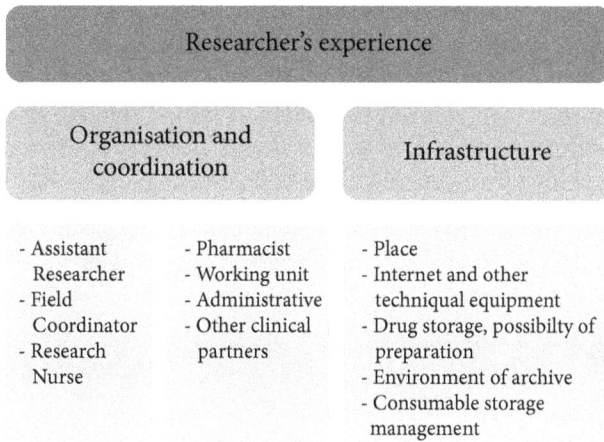

Figure 6: Clinical trial environment requirements

Solutions

Three major issues should be considered to find solutions for the center selection process and the researcher's visibility. The first issue is the regulations on clinical trials by the national health authorities and reflecting them on all institutions involved in clinical trials. The South Korean example should be carefully examined in this respect. South Korea has become one of the leading countries in terms of clinical trials by progressively conducting the central government project for establishing the national infrastructure and centers all around the country, developing recording systems, ensuring continuous training of researchers and other team members, and facilitating the hospitals/institutes to be active components of the project (17). Although many countries in the MENA region began establishing regulations on clinical trials and set goals of increasing clinical trials in their national policies in the early 2000s similar to South Korea, these countries, except for Turkey and Egypt, could not achieve a significant increase in the numbers of clinical trials (4–6). Although the total number of clinical trials in Turkey and Egypt has been quadrupled, it is still less than the number of clinical trials conducted in South Korea. This situation is one of the consequences related to the fact that authority's regulations are not reflected in the sub-units, thereby creating an important barrier. The second issue is providing a research environment and removing the barriers in the institutions where researchers study. According to the results of a survey conducted in Saudi

Arabia, 59.4 % of the researchers stated that they did not feel sufficient institutional support although there were no infrastructure problems (14). The third issue is the leading researchers who will take over the responsibility of the clinical trials and steer the innovative developments. The solution partner of the researcher or the main area that can be at the center of the solution will be their institution and their own individual plans (Figure 1).

1. To be more visible, the researcher should be active in his/her relationships with experienced researchers and sponsor institutions or organizations by taking the following actions:

   a. Participating in meetings or events related to clinical trials
   b. Being a member of national and international organizations related to clinical research
   c. Getting opinions and consultancy from experienced mentors
   d. Participating in the events, such as training and promotional meetings, of sponsor institutions
   e. Participating in the events, such as training and evaluation meetings, held by the health authority
   f. Establishing and/or participating in working groups or professional organizations focused on clinical trials

Table 2 presents the general characteristics of researchers who conduct clinical trials successfully and steadily. Particularly, the factors of a strong commitment and work ethic, the ability to recruit patients, business knowledge and experience, a strong reputation, and networking skills are associated with the researchers' personal characteristics and competence. Intellectual curiosity is a significant motivation that takes the researcher forward in clinical trials. This impulse will be tested by regulatory and logistic hurdles, and the researcher will be able to proceed as long as he/she overcomes them (15, 16, 18).

2. Researchers should not consider clinical trials as part of routine patient follow-ups and treatment programs because of the following features:

   a. Working processes are complex.
   b. Working processes require speed and quality.
   c. Clinical studies are constantly subject to both on-site and online working protocols, compliance with good clinical practice (GCP) guidelines, and quality evaluations.
   d. Clinical studies are time-consuming programs that create a workload due to the numerous requirements, some of which are mentioned here.

e. Unexpected workload and time requirements are inevitable in clinical trials due to developments in the clinical trial processes.

f. The infrastructure of the researcher's institution should be ready for the clinical trials, or the infrastructure should be provided to meet these requirements.

g. It should be considered that the clinical trial processes of other clinics or partners, with which collaboration will be made in the clinical trial, have the capacity to meet the needs and to contribute to the clinical trial.

Due to the increasing workload and time requirement, researchers should be able to make appropriate arrangements in the work environment both in their own clinics and their institutions. For example, they can prepare a workflow chart or coordinate and train the research team to manage the workload in the best way for allocating special time to research in accordance with the intensity of the studies and effective use of this time (14–16,18).

3. Improving the approach of the institutional administrative structure to research activities.

a. In case of an immature clinical trial environment, clinical trials to be conducted may cause anxiety in the patients, physicians, and administrators. It is known that there is a negative attitude toward clinical trials in many countries. It is an important stage for the researcher to express the gains of the clinical trials to all parties in their institution and to minimize the resistances stemming from prejudices (4, 5, 10, 14, 19, 20).

b. Ensuring that the process of initiating the study is carried out in accordance with the specified standards and ensuring the recruitment of trained staff or commissions to the institution.

c. Involving lawyers or legal commissions for legally evaluating the contract processes.

d. Creating the environment and processes in accordance with the requirements of good clinical practice (GCP) (21).

e. Being able to reveal the status of potential subjects suitable for studies at the feasibility stage using the proper software or infrastructure to predict the patient/subject potential.

f. Preparing standard operating procedures for the management of clinical trial processes.

g. Providing the software or organization where potential subjects can be actively monitored during the study process in terms of their eligibility.

h. Arrangement of the clinical trial unit or center in accordance with the GCP.

    i. Storing and preparing the study drugs in accordance with the GCP, and providing suitable environmental conditions before administering them to the patients.

    j. Arrangement of archive conditions in accordance with GCP.

Two factors have a positive influence on the success of the clinical trial: the investigator's experience and site infrastructure support. In countries where the clinical trial environment is not sufficiently mature, the experience and training of the researcher depend on either the opportunities offered by the environment where he/she was trained or his/her commitment to clinical trials (19). In addition, the same is true for infrastructure support. In case no infrastructure has been established before, leading researchers, who will take responsibility and steer the innovative developments, together with the administrators of the institution and other partners, should provide the required infrastructure. After meeting the abovementioned conditions, one of the most critical points that will contribute to the selection of the center is the documentation of the subject potential of the clinical trial and other opportunities of the center. For example, the absence of imaging and laboratory facilities may preclude carrying out a possible clinical trial. Similarly, involving in a study to be carried out with a quite rare subgroup of a low-incidence disease may prove the failure in the beginning.

Characteristics of researchers who have conducted many successful studies (15, 16)

1) sufficient and well-trained staff, particularly clinical research coordinators,
2) institutional support,
3) strong commitment and work ethics,
4) the ability to recruit patients,
5) knowledge and experience in business,
6) a good reputation,
7) networking skills,
8) acting realistically when selecting protocols.

Site Activation
Problems

After the selection of the center and getting permission from the authorities, a site initiation visit (SIV) is paid to the relevant center to initiate the clinical trial. The purpose of the SIV is to review the clinical trial protocol and process, ensure the training of the principal investigator and all members of the research team, and review the equipment inventory of the center regarding the research subject.

In case the general problems and questions mentioned in the center selection section are overcome, usually, no problems will be faced at this stage. On the other hand, in case of involving in a clinical trial before having a mature infrastructure and organization, the researchers and the institution administration will often have difficulty finding solutions for the problems encountered, and it may be a tiring procedure, or it may be impossible to find solutions to the problems. The lack of organization with the administrative and research teams as well as the unmet requirements of the infrastructure and equipment of the center complicate carrying out training and procedures during the SIV.

Solutions

An entrepreneurial and dedicated researcher should anticipate the problems assuming a leading role. They should prevent or minimize the issues before they arise following an approach described in the problems and solutions in the selection of center section.

Volunteer Recruitment
Problems

In the clinical trial process, the sponsor wants to face the accurate result and obtain this result as soon as possible. The delay in delivering an effective and safe drug to patients as soon as possible due to inefficiency is an important problem. Inadequate quality in the performance of the studies sometimes leads to failure in the research on an effective drug. This leads to the inability to access a new treatment option for patients. Also, the delays in the completion of clinical trials and the inefficiency of the centers increase research costs and delay patients' access to drugs (11, 12). As shown in Figure 5,

- 80 % of the studies fall behind the targeted schedule.
- About 20 % of the studies are closed out within a year due to not achieving the targets.
- 18 % of the researchers cannot enroll any patients in the study.
- The cost of opening a center is about 40–45 thousand dollars.
- The five-year cost of non-performing centers is about two billion dollars.
- 20 % of the total cost of clinical trials is wasted.

The above data reveals that in real life, the selection of the center, enrolling eligible patients at the appropriate time while conducting the study in the selected center, and data quality are among the top priorities:

1. Centers engaging in studies that do not cover their own patient populations,
2. Inability to accurately predict patient enrollment potential in centers with not healthy statistics,
3. Researchers' failure to devote enough time to clinical trials and disruption of patient enrollment processes,
4. Not having a systematic workflow in the center to enroll patients in clinical trials, and performing the patient enrollment processes randomly,
5. Failure to select proper eligible patient,
6. Suboptimal administration of the research therapy due to deficiencies in the treatment and side effect management.

The rapid progress and endpoint of clinical trials do not only depend on the screening and enrolment of the subjects. Priorly, initiating clinical trials quickly and concurrently with the world is important. Clinical trials are often carried out by enrolling subjects based on competitions. The delay in the initiation of the study in a country and delay in the activation of the centers will prevent accessing the targeted number of subjects for the centers.

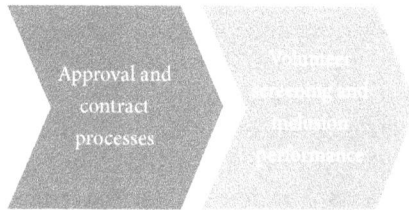

Figure 7: Main factors affecting the pace of clinical trials depending on countries and centers

The issues listed above may negatively affect both patient recruitment and accurate information generation processes (Figure 7). The early dropout of patients from studies particularly due to the ineligibility of the patients included affects study data and results since the clinical trial protocols are not adequately implemented. Occasionally, the pressure of not being able to enroll patients may push researchers in the inexperienced centers to enroll ineligible or controversial patients in the study. Sometimes, for the purpose of being the lead author in a competitive attitude by recruiting more patients or for other expectations, ineligible patients may be enrolled in the study. Enrolling ineligible patients will be deemed a major or critical deviation besides affecting the study results. Due to the resulting performance impairment, the researcher/center is not selected for future studies, and the researcher gives up the clinical trial. Since enrollment of an ineligible patient is a violation of the protocol and the patient gets harmed due to the researched product, it will not be in accordance with the Declaration of Helsinki, GCP, and national regulations; thus, criminal action must be taken against this behavior.

In their study, Adams et al. found that the period until the initiation of the study differed significantly between countries and institutions (20). The period until the initiation of the study is an important performance and eligibility criterion for countries and centers. Researchers working in centers where national and center regulations are not sufficiently suitable will inevitably fall behind in this competitive environment.

On the other hand, in their study, Corneli et al. defined researchers in three categories (16):

✓ Including investigators involved in only one trial ("one-and-done"),
✓ Investigators involved in multiple trials but with substantial intervals between trials ("stop-and-go"),
✓ Investigators continuously involved in multiple trials ("stayers").

Their study revealed that the number of "stayer" researchers has been decreasing both in the US and outside the US over time, whereas the number of "one-and-done" researchers has been increasing. On the other hand, Fordyces et al. (15) listed the reasons why "one-and-done" researchers did not conduct more studies as follows:

✓ Workload balance
✓ Time requirements
✓ Data and safety reporting
✓ Finance-related issues

These results reveal that the intensive work schedule and the need for time discourage many researchers from conducting research. The same studies reported that the number of "one-and-done" researchers has increased over the years and reached about 8000 globally in 2015. However, the number of "stayer" researchers has decreased over the years and declined below 2000. Considering the factors that make researchers reluctant for the clinical trials and the factors that ensure their continuity and success, it seems that the dedication and entrepreneurial characteristics of the researcher, infrastructure, institutional support, and the training and competence of team members are the main factors related to the research process.

Solutions

In countries where the clinical research environment is not sufficiently developed, taking over the heavy workload of clinical trials without infrastructure, administrative support, and team support to share jobs may be daunting for researchers in time, or they are not regarded as a priority center and researcher by the sponsor due to the disruptions in the processes. In these environments, the researcher can solve many infrastructural and organizational deficiencies with his/her own efforts through proactive actions and information exchange with the administrative team and other in-house clinical research partners. Researchers' integration with the world, foresight, and entrepreneurship can play a decisive role in undeveloped geographies. With the awareness of clinical trials in their previous study environments, the researchers can provide significant contributions to the regulations that are not mature yet. Therefore, being aware of international and national regulations on clinical trials and ensuring their self-development are important for researchers to improve clinical trial environments.

1. It is important for them to achieve a selective, effective, and ethical work pace by considering the determinations about clinical center performances given in Figure 4.
2. Resolving contracts and other approval processes quickly in the center.
3. Continuous monitoring of the status of potential subjects suitable for studies using appropriate software or infrastructures to predict the patient/subject potential.
4. Developing standard operating procedures for the management of clinical research processes.
5. Providing software or organization where potential subjects can be actively monitored during the study process regarding their eligibility for the study.
6. The center should have a systematic approach for patient screening and enrollment processes, and this process should not be left to individual effort.
7. Ensuring that each member of the study team has sufficient training on their study duties and takes an active role during the study period.

Thus, patient screening and enrolment processes will be carried out in order in the center.

Informed Consent, Visits, and Patient Follow-Ups

Problems Regarding ICF

In the clinical trial process, informing the patients as per the Declaration of Helsinki (23) and the GCP (21), the willingness of the patient to the research, and issuing its document (ICF) are the first and most crucial stages in the enrolment of the subject in the study. The ICF should be signed by the researcher and the subject in a standardized manner by allocating a special time. The Principal Investigator (PI) or the researcher delegated by the PI informs the patient and gives him/her the necessary time to read, think, and evaluate the ICF. In environments where the workload is high and clinical trials are deemed to be carried out by working into other activities, or where the regulations on patient rights and responsibilities cannot be applied under universal conditions, consent processes using ICF may not be performed in accordance with GCP (20).

Problems related to ICF are regarded as critical deviations, and they will expose researchers to legal liabilities that include penal sanctions.

Solutions Regarding ICF

1. Special time and environment should be allocated for issuing ICF.
2. Adequate time should be provided to the patient for the interview. Since this period may vary from patient to patient, the informing process should not be carried out in limited times.
3. A free and comfortable environment should be provided to the patient for giving information and reading the ICF, thinking over and evaluating the processes, and expressing the questions they want to ask.
4. The patient should not be obliged to sign the ICF or give consent in a limited time and in an environment where he/she is not comfortable.
5. The consent process should be carried out before the researchers, and it should not be left to non-research team members.
6. Attention should be paid to the definitions of restricted subjects defined in national and international regulations.
7. The literacy of the subject should be considered, and appropriate procedures should be implemented for those who are illiterate or unable to sign.
8. The friends or relatives of the subject shall not be allowed to sign the ICF on behalf of the subject.
9. The ICFs shall be kept securely, and a certified and signed copy shall be given to the subject.

10.The details about the center and the researcher on the ICF should be checked each time whether they are correct.

11.Preparing standard operating procedures (SOPs) for the abovementioned and several other applications and training team members on these procedures are the most applicable ways to manage the workload and probable errors.

Problems Regarding Patient Visits and Follow-Up

Many researchers, in addition to their other responsibilities, must devote time to clinical trials. Workflow charts may be extremely intense, especially when job descriptions and time schedules are ambiguous. One of the most frequently encountered difficulties is conducting patient visits while performing routine daily tasks (Figure 8). It should be kept in mind that our daily practice should be carried out within the framework of the patient–doctor relationship in accordance with the national and institutional regulations binding us.

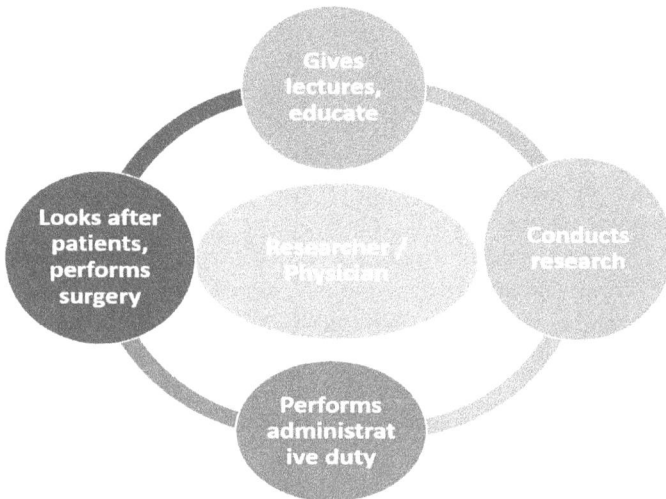

Figure 8: Workload of research physicians

On the other hand, in the clinical trials, the patient treatment must be carried out in accordance to the clinical trial protocol of a newly researched product ensuring real-time coordination with many in-house and external partners in line with a plan requiring many record systems. As shown in Figure 9, it is necessary to coordinate with multiple clinical research team members concurrently, maintain communication with various institutions, and record all developments in real-time in a detailed, intelligible, and explanatory manner. Quality, accountability, and transparency issues may arise due to delays in conducting these processes, inadequate data generation for clinical trials, failure to perform these processes thoroughly, and failure to be comprehensible, detailed, and explanatory.

The well-being and safety of subjects are the top priority in clinical trials (21–23). Safety assessment of newly used products on humans and the application of safe transportation and storage of researched products are among the major issues to be focused on in a clinical trial center.

Following issues may cause important problems:

1. Not assigning adequate and dedicated time for clinical studies and patient visits,
2. Failure to prepare special settings for clinical studies and patient visits,
3. Lack of familiarity between the researcher and the research team with the study protocols and study treatment procedures,
4. The researcher physicians' proclivity to maintain habits inconsistent with clinical research protocols throughout the clinical research process,
5. Failure to pay attention to protocol updates,
6. Inadequate documentation during patient visits in clinical studies,
7. Specifying the roles and responsibilities of the qualified site coordinator, and his/her training,
8. Specifying the roles and responsibilities of the assistant researcher, and his/her training,
9. Specifying the roles and responsibilities of the research nurse, and his/her training,
10. Specifying the roles and responsibilities of the research pharmacists, and his/her training,
11. Specifying the roles and responsibilities of other members of the clinical research team, and their training,
12. Transfer, storage, administration, and waste tracking of the study drugs,
13. Storage of study and patient documents and other materials (Figure 9).

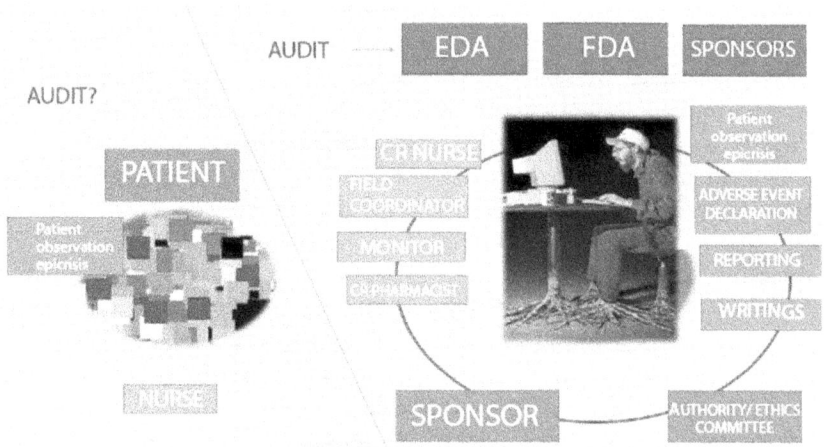

Figure 9: Differences between daily routine patient care and patient care in clinical trials

Solutions Regarding Patient Visits and Follow-Up (24, 25)

The researchers should keep in mind that clinical trials are not a one-man show. The solution can be obtained by ensuring sufficient time, appropriate environment, good implementation of the main principles of teamwork, and implementing the GCP guidelines thoroughly.

1. Sufficient time should be allocated for each patient.
2. Patient visits should be conducted in an environment prepared in accordance with the nature of clinical trials.
3. It is essential for the researcher to have a good knowledge of the rationale, design, protocol content, and management of the administered treatment during the clinical trial. Knowing the research protocol in detail, knowing the efficacy, safety, and administration properties of the researched drugs adequately, and administering them properly will ensure minimizing protocol deviations and problems faced during patient management processes.
4. It is crucial to know the practices standardized with the clinical trial protocol and researcher brochures and carrying out the patient management in accordance with the study protocol. Keeping fewer records and changing standards according to the patient and physician approaches in daily practices are not valid for clinical studies while testing the efficacy and safety of a newly tested product in humans. In clinical trials, the physician should administer the

research products properly to the patient group that meets the inclusion and exclusion criteria in accordance with the study protocol. Administrations cannot be changed depending on the patient and the physician's approach unless a particular situation arises.

5. Research protocols are updated according to developments or interim analyses during clinical studies. When researchers and centers receive these updates, they should be evaluated immediately, and research team members should be informed and trained on these issues. This will prevent errors throughout the study and during the visits in the face of the current situation.

6. All research team members should document developments in an intelligible, detailed, and explanatory manner in real-time, and these procedures should be checked periodically by the principal investigator or the delegated assistant researchers.

7. It is very important to qualify the site coordinator and other clinical study team members in environments where the clinical study culture has not been sufficiently developed. Therefore, basic and advanced GCP training should be taken and updated from time to time. Training programs should be provided periodically for all staff in the clinical trial center for each study and adverse events and other developments in the study process, and defects identified in the monitoring or audits.

8. Obtaining sufficient information about the efficacy and safety of newly researched products before the study, having a good knowledge of the protocol about the side effects and managing them, and following up the data on the product that is constantly updated are highly essential for the researcher. Special attention is required due to the lack of general experience with these newly tested drugs on humans; also, reporting and defining these issues contribute to the formation of important information about the product.

It is the sponsor's responsibility to ensure that research products are safely transported to the research center. However, the responsibility of receiving, storing, occasional transfers in the center, and administering them to the subject belong to the center and the researcher. SOPs should be specified for each stage. Multiple control systems and alternative plans should be prepared due to the disruptions, and these issues should be specified in the SOPs. Training the team members and preparing their job descriptions accordingly can prevent problems such as heat deviation of research products, quarantine on drugs, disruption of patient visits and treatments, and major/critical deviations (Figure 10).

9. Keeping the records of all the training programs performed, and the outputs obtained from the training programs and experiences, preparing and updating

the SOPs that will provide the basis for the operation of the research center, and arranging the roles and responsibilities of the team members in accordance with these SOPs will facilitate the processes of the center and improve the quality.

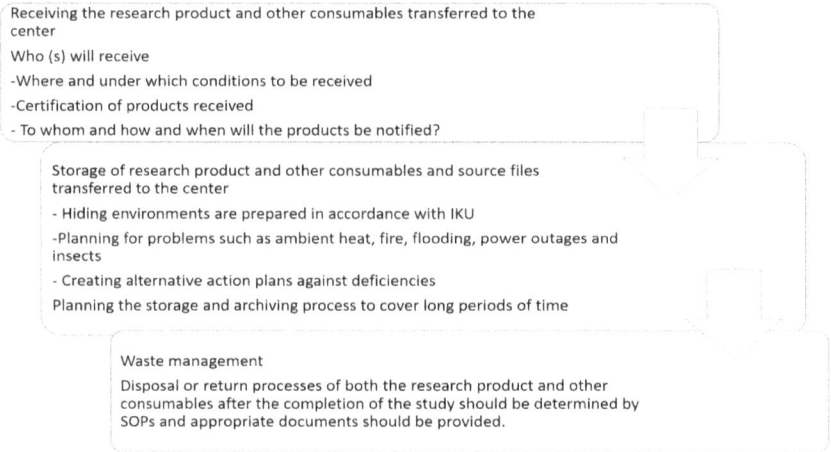

Receiving the research product and other consumables transferred to the center

Who (s) will receive

-Where and under which conditions to be received

-Certification of products received

- To whom and how and when will the products be notified?

Storage of research product and other consumables and source files transferred to the center

- Hiding environments are prepared in accordance with IKU

-Planning for problems such as ambient heat, fire, flooding, power outages and insects

- Creating alternative action plans against deficiencies

Planning the storage and archiving process to cover long periods of time

Waste management

Disposal or return processes of both the research product and other consumables after the completion of the study should be determined by SOPs and appropriate documents should be provided.

Figure 10: Action plan recommendations for research products, consumables and resource files

Monitoring, Inspection, and Quality (24–28)
Problems

As shown in Figure 9, one of the most critical aspects of the clinical trials is preparing intelligible, detailed, and explanatory documentation in line with GCP in close collaboration with sponsors and authorities and subject to their assessment and supervision. The monitoring process is important in ensuring compliance with the study protocol, detecting and eliminating any shortcomings, and keeping the research team ready for the study.

Monitoring is defined as "the act of overseeing the progress of a clinical trial, and ensuring that it is conducted, recorded, and reported following the protocol, standard operating procedures (SOPs), GCP, and the applicable regulatory requirement(s)" [ICH 1.38].

Quality Control (QC) is defined as "the operational techniques and activities undertaken within the quality assurance system to verify that the requirements for quality of the trial-related activities are fulfilled" [ICH 1.47].

The term "audit" is defined as "a systematic and independent examination of trial-related activities and documents to determine whether the evaluated trial-related activities were conducted, and the data were recorded, analyzed, and accurately reported according to the protocol, sponsor's standard operating procedures (SOPs), GCP, and the applicable regulatory requirement(s)" [ICH 1.6].

Inspections are the audits conducted by health authorities such as the FDA and EMA in research centers to evaluate the reliability and accuracy of the data they offer.

1. Researchers failing to devote enough time for monitoring procedures performed by the sponsor and performing monitoring procedures with the initiative of less competent team members.
2. Failure to prepare a suitable environment for monitoring.
3. Monitoring procedures are typically carried out by non-physician Clinical Research Assistants (CRAs). As a result, they often cause misunderstandings, as well as incomplete and erroneous assessments and guidance.
4. In environments where the clinical research culture is immature, the monitoring process can turn into an intervention in the clinical trial process rather than a conformity assessment.
5. In environments where the clinical research culture is immature, monitors, with the concern of making errors due to uncertainties, may demand unnecessary things that will increase the workload of the research center and the researcher.
6. Unlike monitoring, the audit inspects practices of the research center and the researcher, as well as the sponsor in that center. Therefore, monitoring responsibilities of the center and researchers are also applicable for the audit procedures.
7. Inspection can be viewed as a type of audit carried out by the health authorities.
8. The findings of the inspections and audits may enforce sanctions that can lead to the disqualification of the researchers in the centers from further studies.

The problems arising in this section are actually the problems that cover all the responsibilities of the center and the researcher; therefore, they will not be discussed again in detail. The problems that could be reported to the researcher and the center by the monitoring and audit parties were highlighted.

Solutions

The researchers can develop solutions for the emerging problems using their general knowledge as well as their knowledge, experience, and training on the clinical studies. The responsible party for the findings of audits and inspections is the researcher, not the center. In other words, a sanction that may arise binds the relevant principal investigator. For example, a critical finding detected in the FDA inspection is filed against the principal investigator; other researchers at that center are not affected by this situation. Researchers should keep in mind that they can delegate some tasks to team members; however, they cannot delegate their responsibilities. Therefore, the researcher is at the center of the solution and responsibilities. The center's responsibilities also belong to the researcher because the researcher declares the eligibility of the center in terms of GCP, other requirements, and equipment in his/her evaluations before entering the study. In other words, the researcher is accepted to the study because he/she declares that his/her center is eligible for the proposed research, thus bears the responsibility.

1. The center must be prepared to meet the GCP requirements and other equipment requirements for the clinical trial.
2. Suitable environments should be prepared for monitoring and inspection procedures.
3. The basic condition for the organizations and solutions is that researchers should have a good knowledge of national and international regulations, ethical rules, particularly the Declaration of Helsinki and GCP guidelines.
4. Extreme interventions of the sponsor can be eliminated by the competency of the investigator.
5. Preliminary preparation may be required for audits and inspections. It will be beneficial for researchers to be knowledgeable about these issues and to get support from experienced researchers and centers.
6. The clinical trial has a universal culture, so the evolution of our local habits into this universal culture is quite important for the standardization of the clinical trial and patient care.
7. Researcher and center practices should be constantly improved both by changing the habits and gaining experience from each study in line with the results of monitoring and audits.

8. Preparing SOPs for each field for the center and researcher practices and updating them according to new situations, and the compliance of team members with the SOPs are among the most important steps for standardization.

Authoring, Steering / Executive Committee Member

One of the most important contributions of clinical studies to researchers is the national and international reputation.

1. Many researchers imagine being a co-author or perhaps a lead author in their research paper. While enrolling a high number of patients in clinical studies is a notable criterion, it is often not sufficient.
2. Being a steering/executive committee member is an achievement that is entirely based on the performance shown during the clinical trials and academic reputation over time.

In addition to the factors of enrolling a high number of patients and the relations with the sponsor about the developments in both patients and procedures during the study, the researchers' suggestions that may even contribute to the study protocol from time to time may pave the way of researchers to come forefront for the authorship. However, authorship policies may differ according to the sponsor, or they may differ from one study to another. Authorship policies are often defined ambiguously, and they can be changed during the study. Being aware of these issues may offer advantages to the researchers (29).

Being a steering/executive committee member is an achievement that may arise as academic reputation improves in time during the clinical trial.

Academic entrepreneurship, high quality and ethical performance, and good networking capabilities facilitate the researchers' prominence.

Studies Initiated by the Researcher (30)

Attention should be paid to the differences between the definitions presented in Figure 11 to define and understand the studies initiated by the researcher in terms of clinical trials.

Clinical Studies - Definitions

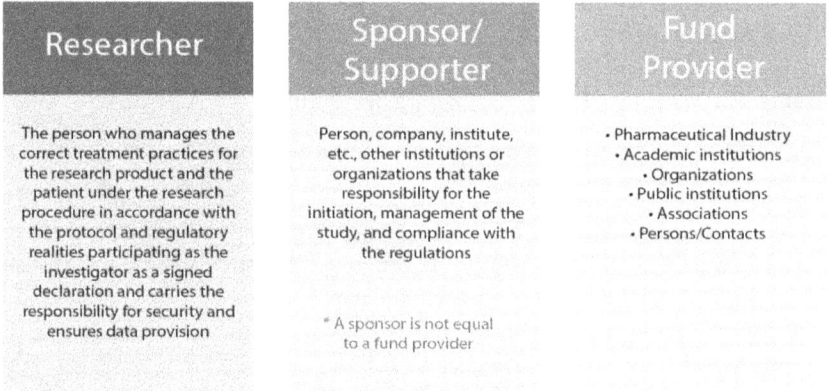

Researcher	Sponsor/ Supporter	Fund Provider
The person who manages the correct treatment practices for the research product and the patient under the research procedure in accordance with the protocol and regulatory realities participating as the investigator as a signed declaration and carries the responsibility for security and ensures data provision	Person, company, institute, etc., other institutions or organizations that take responsibility for the initiation, management of the study, and compliance with the regulations * A sponsor is not equal to a fund provider	• Pharmaceutical Industry • Academic institutions • Organizations • Public institutions • Associations • Persons/Contacts

Figure 11: Researcher, sponsor, and fund provider definitions in the clinical research process

As can be understood from the definitions, the terms "sponsor" and "fund provider" have different meanings. Sponsor and fund provider may be the same party particularly in the industry-supported studies (Figure 11). In academic studies, private institutions, public institutions, and associations themselves, or the industry, may be the sponsor and fund provider. Among these two clinical research parties, the role of researchers in the center is to carry out the study in their own unit. However, in clinical studies initiated by the researcher, the researcher becomes a sponsor researcher after obtaining funds from different fund providers similar to academic studies. Therefore, the researcher has the responsibility for the whole process from the design of the study to the publication. Therefore, the sponsor researcher is responsible for the management of all logistics, technical, and other processes such as establishing the study protocol, obtaining permission from the authorities and ethics committees, and organizing the center or centers.

Therefore, the studies initiated by the researcher in environments that do not have a clinical research culture are quite limited and even ignored (Figure 12). Moreover, the management of the process can be quite challenging. The process can be managed by a Contract Research Organization (CRO); otherwise, it will be very difficult for the researchers to overcome the mentioned challenges of industry-supported studies. This field makes significant contributions to medical applications. Industry-supported clinical studies are very important in terms of gaining research experience and the development of researcher culture. Reflecting their experiences in this field to the investigator-initiated research (IIR), the clinical research culture, and its successive gains are critical for the researchers themselves, their teams, and nations.

Researcher initiated clinical trials

Clinical Research- Research

Sector/Other	Researcher
Studies on the development of drugs and treatments are often thought to be under the responsibility / control of the pharmaceutical industry.	•Independent, patient-focused, researcher-led, guided studies •Plays an important role in improving patient's treatments

Researcher initiated study
Researcher driven study
Physician led study
Researcher sponsored

Figure 12: Studies initiated by the researcher are different from the studies initiated by the industry

Since IIR is a separate topic, it will not be discussed further in this section. As it is an important subject to be kept in mind, it is reasonably discussed here.

Other

Qualified Personal

In countries where clinical research environments are not mature yet, one of the most fundamental problems is the qualified staff. It can take time and be a problem for the clinical study staff of the sponsor and CROs as well as the research center's investigator, assistant researcher, site coordinator, nurse, pharmacist, and other staff to gain the required discipline and competence even if they have been trained. Particularly, the high turnover frequency of the staff may cause problems in terms of continuity due to the short-term stay of many staff in the same project.

Contact

Due to the lack of standards in communication between researchers both within their own institutions (administration, other clinics, commissions, ethics committee) and between clinical study partners at the national level (authority, ethics committee, professional organizations, sponsors, CROs, etc.), there may be ups and downs depending on people. Particularly, keeping the communication channels open is critical for solving problems and ensuring progress in the stages where clinical trial progresses.

Prejudice

Prejudice of the citizens, physicians, administrators, and authorities against clinical trials may build an important barrier in conducting research in many countries. In order to cope with prejudices, researchers should inform their colleagues, community, and the authority both in their institutions and at the national level about the outcomes of the clinical trials, and their effects on the wellbeing of the patient.

Clinical Research and R&D

There are ongoing discussions in many countries whether clinical trials are R&D or not. Frascati Manual 2015 clearly highlights that clinical trial is an R&D as an experimental development, and it states the definitions and regulations in explicit expressions in several sections (31).

Researcher and Corporate Payments

The regulation on the researcher payments varies even in developed countries. Because of the fact that national regulations do not set regulatory rules on this issue, the researchers are exposed to the different initiatives of institutional administrations. Even the same institution may apply different payment policies in a short period. The basic solution in this issue is that the national authority should make regulations that will not allow too much difference in this developing field.

Since the lack of standardization and presence of uncertainties in institution and service payments may prevent making budget projections, this may cause the sponsors not to offer research to the country or institutions. Ensuring standardization in the service pricing of the institutions and avoiding unjustified changes is important both for the national level and institutions.

References

1. https://ourworldindata.org/world-population-growth   (access   date, 12.08.2020).

2. https://www.unicef.org/mena/media/4141/file/MENA-Gen2030.pdf   (access date, 12.08.2020).

3. https://clinicaltrials.gov/ct2/search/map/click?map.x=660&map.y= 450&mapw=1879 (access date, 12.08.2020).

4. The evolving clinical research environment in MENA region – Jordan as a case study Ahmad Arouri Master Thesis, May 2014.

5. Erdogan B, Seker O, Chin LV. Regulations and recruitment: Experiences in the Middle East. Journal for Clinical Studies. 2017;9(3):30–34.

6. https://www.iqvia.com/locations/middle-east-and-africa/library/white-pap ers/unearthing-the-potential-of-clinical-trial-market-in-mena (access date, 12.08.2020).

7. https://www.fda.gov/files/science%20%26%20research/published/9-45--- 11-00-Investigator-Responsibilities-%E2%80%93-Regulation-and-Clinical- Trials.pdf (access date 20.07.2020).

8. https://www.fda.gov/media/78830/download (access date 20.07.2020).

9. Unger JM, Nghiem VT, Hershman DL, Vaidya R, LeBlanc M, Blanke CD. Association of National Cancer Institute-Sponsored Clinical Trial Network Group Studies With Guideline Care and New Drug Indications. JAMA Netw Open. 2019;2(9):e1910593. Published 2019 Sep 4. doi:10.1001/ jamanetworkopen.2019.10593.

10. https://catalyst.harvard.edu/pdf/regulatory/Sponsor-InvestigatorFrequetl yAskedQuestions.pdf (access date 20.07.2020).

11. Getz KA, Wenger J, Campo RA, Seguine ES, Kaitin KI. Assessing the Impact of Protocol Design Changes on Clinical Trial Performance. Am J Ther. 2008;15(5):450–457. doi:10.1097/MJT.0b013e31816b9027.

12. Koçkaya G, Demir M, Kockaya PD, Tatar M, Üresin AY. Economic Impact of Clinical Research to Research Centers and Opportunity Cost for the Reimbursement System in Turkey. Health. 2015;07:1124–1133.

13. Getz K. Improving Protocol Design Feasibility to Drive Drug Development Economics and Performance. Int J Environ Res Public Health. 2014;11:5069–5080.

14. Sulthan N. Perception of Clinical Research among Clinical Investigators in Saudi Arabia. Asian J Pharm Clin Res. 2015;8(3);243–246.

15. Fordyce CB, Malone K, Forrest A, et al. Improving and Sustaining the Site Investigator Community: Recommendations from the Clinical Trials

Transformation Initiative. Contemp Clin Trials Commun. 2019;16:100462. Published 2019 Oct 17. doi:10.1016/j.conctc.2019.100462.

16. Corneli A, Pierre C, Hinkley T, et al. One and Done: Reasons Principal Investigators Conduct Only One FDA-Regulated Drug Trial. Contemp Clin Trials Commun. 2017;6:31–38. Published 2017 Mar 8. doi:10.1016/j.conctc.2017.02.009.

17. Chee DH. Korean Clinical Trials: Its Current Status, Future Prospects, and Enabling Environment. Transl Clin Pharmacol. 2019;27(4):115–118. doi:10.12793/tcp.2019.27.4.115.

18. Tohid H, Choudhury SM, Agouba S, et al. Perceptions and Attitudes to Clinical Research Participation in Qatar. Contemp Clin Trials Commun. 2017;8:241–247. Published 2017 Nov 1. doi:10.1016/j.conctc.2017.10.010.

19. Nair SC, Ibrahim H, Celentano DD. Clinical Trials in the Middle East and North Africa (MENA) Region: Grandstanding or Grandeur?. Contemp Clin Trials. 2013;36(2):704–710. doi:10.1016/j.cct.2013.05.009.

20. Adams MCB, Bicket MC, Murphy JD, Wu CL, Hurley RW. Opportunities and Challenges for Junior Investigators Conducting Pain Clinical Trials. Pain Rep. 2019;4(3):e639. doi:10.1097/PR9.0000000000000639.

21. https://ichgcp.net/ (access date 14.08.2020).

22. World Medical Association. World Medical Association Declaration of Helsinki: Ethical Principles for M<edical Research Involving Human Subjects. JAMA. 2013;310(20):2191–2194. doi:10.1001/jama.2013.281053.

23. https://www.wma.net/policies-post/wma-declaration-of-helsinki-ethical-principles-for-medical-research-involving-human-subjects/ (access date, 13.08.202).

24. https://florencehc.com/go/download-link-guide-to-monitoring-in-clinical-trials/ (access date, 13.08.2020).

25. https://www.georgiacancerinfo.org/images/public/embedded/SS-204.01%20Site%20Initiation%20Visit.pdf (access date, 13.08.2020).

26. Ravi R, Bose D, Gogtay NJ, Thatte UM. Investigator Preparedness for Monitoring and Audits. Perspect Clin Res. 2018;9(2):95–98. doi:10.4103/picr.PICR_42_18.

27. https://ccrod.cancer.gov/confluence/download/attachments/71041052/Monitoring_auditing6.pdf?version=1&modificationDate=1317305516223 (access date, 13.08.2020).

28. https://www.fda.gov/media/93884/download (access date 20.07.2020).

29. Marušić A, Hren D, Mansi B, et al. Five-Step Authorship Framework to Improve Transparency in Disclosing Contributors to Industry-Sponsored

Clinical Trial Publications. BMC Med. 2014;12:197. Published 2014 Oct 24. doi:10.1186/s12916-014-0197-z.

30. http://www.crc.gov.my/wp-content/uploads/2016/07/02_iit_made_easy_2 015.pdf (access date, 13.08.2020.

31. OECD. Frascati Manual 2015: Guidelines for Collecting and Reporting Data on Research and Experimental Development. Paris: OECD Publishing, 2015.

Peri Aytaç, Aydın Erenmemişoğlu

Early Phase Clinical Trials – Importance of Entry to MENA

Clinical trials consist of five phases: Early Phase I (formerly Phase 0) to Phase IV. While first three phases (Early Phase I to Phase II) are described as Early Phase Trials, Phase III and IV are named as Late Phase Trials (1). These phases described briefly as follows.

Early Phase I (formerly Phase 0): This phase does not aim therapeutic or diagnostic results, and the basic goal of this phase is whether study drug is affecting the body. These exploratory trials are conducted before Phase I trials including very limited human subjects (1).

Phase I: This phase aims at exhibiting safety of the study drug. It is usually conducted with a small number of healthy participants and targets to describe tolerability, safety, pharmacokinetics, pharmacodynamics, food or drug interactions, differences between age groups or gender, or relative bioavailability of different formulation of the research molecule (1, 2).

Basically Phase 0 and Phase I studies are "First in Human" studies, and they are the key step for new drug development (2). Phase I clinical research studies last mostly for several months, and it is reported of approximately consisting 14.1 % of total clinical research investment and 8.7 % of the R&D investment, while 70 % of experimental drugs studied in Phase I proceed to Phase II, in global (3).

Due to the current legislations, Phase I studies should be conducted at Phase I clinical research centers which is approved by the official authorities. In Turkey, these phase I clinical research sites must get their approval from Republic of Turkey Ministry of Health Turkish Medicines and Medical Devices Agency-(*Türkiye İlaç ve Tıbbi Cihaz Kurumu-TİTCK*).

Phase II: This phase aims at gathering preliminary data on whether the study drug is efficient in a group of participants who have a certain condition/disease. This population size may reach up to several hundreds of patients. Phase II studies are generally conducted with a comparison group (e.g., placebo or existing treatment). Safety issues are also continued to be monitored and evaluated together with adverse events (1).

It is declared that while individual Phase II studies generally last only several weeks or months, the entire studies conducted in Phase II may take several months to two years. Currently, Phase II clinical research consists of 18.8 % of total clinical research investment and 11.6 % of the overall R&D investment, while about 33 % of experimental drugs in this phase proceed to late phase study, Phase III (3).

Focusing on some certain zones, Middle East and North Africa (MENA) region is hosting nearly half a billion of people which means 6 % of the world population and according to a published data about MENA Clinical Trials Market Analysis, the value of the region was 1.36 billion dollars in 2020 (4).

As of today, the research-driven zones such as United States and Europe take the biggest share of early phase studies, by 55 % and 23 %, respectively. Together with Korea and Australia, these regions consist only 14 % of the world population, while dominating the number of early phase trials. In contrary to this, countries located in MENA region take quite smaller share of these trials. Excluding Israel, Turkey, and Egypt take the biggest share of this region, approximately with 0.6 % and 0.9 %, respectively. Even though clinicaltrials.gov data may not reflect the actual or correct numbers, these data may give an overall interpretation about active studies worldwide, and the share of this region consists of a very narrow part of the market. Extracted data reflect the number of studies of following options selected: (i) already recruiting; (ii) not yet recruiting; (iii) active but not recruiting; or (iv) enrolling by invitation, for all charts and tables below (5).

Table 1: Worldwide distribution of actively conducted early phase studies by countries (%)

Countries	Worldwide Distribution of Early Phase Studies (%)
The United States	54.52
Europe	16.44
The United Kingdom	5.97
Australia	4.06
Korea	3.82
Israel	1.78
Egypt	0.87
Turkey	0.58
Iran	0.19
Jordan	0.18
Lebanon	0.14
Saudi Arabia	0.19

Source: clinicaltrials.gov

Taking at a glance to share of early phase studies conducting worldwide by phase (Table 2), it can be seen that in the US, the percent of early phase I (phase 0) studies which are conducted currently are higher than the other early-phase trials. Surprisingly, Egypt exhibits a similar situation and leaves a number of developed countries behind in respect to early Phase I (Phase 0) studies which are being conducted currently in the country. Among MENA countries, Egypt owns the highest share followed by Turkey in respect to Phase II studies (5).

Table 2: The share of countries conducting early phase studies by phase

Countries	Early Phase I	Phase I	Phase II
The United States	62.78	58.70	51.36
Europe	0.31	9.91	21.63
The United Kingdom	1.22	5.98	6.36
Australia	0.46	4.75	3.94
Korea	0.38	3.64	4.20
Israel	0.76	1.39	2.10
Egypt	2.44	0.60	0.91
Turkey	0.08	0.25	0.81
Iran	0.08	0.17	0.22
Jordan	0.00	0.20	0.18
Lebanon	0.08	0.02	0.21
Saudi Arabia	0.15	0.11	0.24

Source: clinicaltrials.gov

Despite the location (proximity to Europe and MENA regions both), infrastructure, and well-established clinical trial environment including GCP-trained investigators and staff, Turkey still has a very low share in early phase clinical trials. Considering the originator companies generally conduct first phase trials where their company is located; the main reason of Turkey's backwardness may be the lack of development of an original molecule so far. However, patient population and fast result–providing capacity with high data quality make Turkey very attractive in Phase II clinical trials (3).

Tremendous potential of MENA in terms of treatment-naïve population, low-cost budgets, and well-established hospitalization facilities draw attention towards global pharmaceutical industry. Collaborating with the policy makers of the countries such as Egypt, Jordan, Saudi Arabia, United Arab Emirates, Lebanon, and Algeria, this region became very attractive for industrial-based sponsors conducting clinical trials. However, some safety concerns still limit conducting early-phase studies in some countries of this region (6). This situation creates a massive opportunity for Turkey to involve MENA region and collaborate with professionals in this field.

Moreover, Turkey's well-established clinical research regulation and regulatory authority, TITCK, which is already a full member of International Committee of Harmonization (ICH), works in compliance with European Medicines Agency. Besides, there are laws and enforcements including "Personal Data Protecting Law," which are effectively conducted in order to protect all parties of trial participants. Besides, online submission system and fast approval rate or feedbacks of TITCK make Turkey an attractive country for the global companies operating in the region (3).

Turkey currently has thirteen authority-approved Phase I clinical centers which are already conducting or ready to run first-in-human trials and this number grows fast. These sites are listed below:

- Ankara City Hospital Clinical Research Center*
- ARGEFAR-Ege University Drug Development and Pharmacokinetic Research-Application Center*
- Çam ve Sakura Clinical Research Center
- Dokuz Eylül University Phase 1 Clinical Research Center
- Ege University, Faculty of Medicine Children's Hospital, Pediatric Hamatology Clinic
- Erciyes University Hakan Çetinsaya Good Clinical Practice and Research Center*
- Gazi University Hospital Department of Child Metabolism
- Koç University Hospital Phase 1 Research Center
- Sağlık Bilimleri University, Adana City Training and Research Hospital Phase 1 Clinical Research Center
- Sağlık Bilimleri University, Ankara Abdurrahman Yurtaslan Oncology Training and Research Hospital Phase 1 Center
- Sağlık Bilimleri University İstanbul Mehmet Akif Ersoy Thoracic and Cardiovascular Surgery Training and Research Hospital
- Selçuk University Good Clinical Practice and Research Center
- Yeditepe University R&D and Analysis Center*
- * These centers are also serving as BE/BA Centers.

MENA region and Turkey are known to have high prevalence in terms of rare diseases and genetic conditions (7). Rare diseases are still an untapped area of drug discovery field, and these regions present a great opportunity to develop novel treatments for such conditions. Abovementioned centers are not only fully equipped to conduct clinical studies and enhance the early phase trial share of Turkey in the region, but also they are ready to collaborate for innovative research with the centers in MENA.

Patients who suffer from rare diseases are also eager to participate in trials. By reaching more patient population, awareness about clinical trials in the society will improve and let further improvements both in scientific and financial aspects.

Together with rare diseases, prevalence of Type-II diabetes, obesity, cardio-vascular diseases are increasing remarkably in some MENA countries with growing economy as well (6). While the need for potent treatments in MENA is still unmet, accompanied by Turkey, this will lead to innovative paths in terms of clinical trials. It is estimated that the strong background of Turkey, especially in Phase II trials, will make the biggest contribution to studies conducted in MENA region (3, 5).

On the Chart 1 and Table 3, it can be seen that the number of Phase II trials takes the biggest share worldwide and by country in early phase trials when distributing within itself. Especially Turkey exhibits a remarkable percentile for Phase II. This distribution basically portrays the strength of Turkey for studies initially conducted on focused patient population. In addition to this, if research-based and innovator pharmaceutical industry is encouraged to run their first-in-human studies while taking advantage of Turkey's facility and investigative infrastructure, Turkish pharmaceutical industry could easily dominate the MENA region.

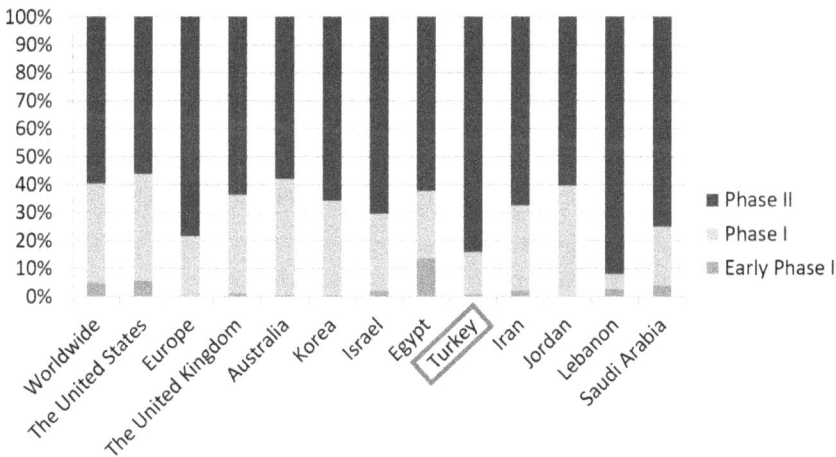

Figure 1: Distribution of early phase trials worldwide and within certain countries
Source: clinicaltrials.gov

Table 3: Distribution of early phase trials conducted worldwide and within certain countries

Distribution of Early Phase Studies by Phase (%)	Early Phase I	Phase I	Phase II
Worldwide	4.81	35.55	59.64
The United States	5.54	38.27	56.19
Europe	0.09	21.43	78.48
The United Kingdom	0.98	35.57	63.45
Australia	0.54	41.59	57.87
Korea	0.48	33.91	65.61
Israel	2.06	27.78	70.16
Egypt	13.45	24.37	62.18
Turkey	0.64	15.29	84.08
Iran	1.92	30.77	67.31
Jordan	0.00	39.58	60.42
Lebanon	2.70	5.41	91.89
Saudi Arabia	3.85	21.15	75.00

Source: clinicaltrials.gov

Not only first-in-human studies but also bioequivalence/bioavailability (BE/BA) studies are included in Phase I trials. Estimated value of BE/BA studies in Turkey is 8 USD million annually as of 2020. These studies lead considerable contribution of Turkish generic pharmaceutical manufacturers to various drug markets and help transforming Turkey a crucial actor of the sector. In Turkey, currently there are six authority-approved research centers conducting BE/BA studies, serving for clinical and/or bioanalytical studies.

The list for BE/BA Clinics and Bioanalytical Centers in Turkey is given below, together with previously mentioned centers with asterisk (*) above:

- FARMAGEN Good Clinical Practice Center
- Istanbul University Drug Application and Research Center
- Novagenix Bioanalytical Drug R&D Center

Recent COVID-19 pandemic situation devastatingly proved the importance of clinical trials. During the pandemic, almost all clinical studies were affected negatively and some of them had to be terminated early. Under these circumstances the bioequivalence studies of the pandemic medications (favipiravir, lopinavir/ritonavir) were conducted for license and availability. Not only for Turkey but also worldwide, those studies have been a unique experience for conducting

Phase I level studies in terms of safety and risk during the pandemic and added a notable value in terms of access to treatment during extraordinary situations.

Emerging economies such as Turkey, Egypt, UAE, and others located at MENA region give a giant opportunity for innovation-driven companies of the pharmaceutical sector in terms of patient population, legislative regulations, competitive costs, facility, and investigative infrastructures. While the numbers of early phase R&D studies are limited so far, there's a huge chance for success for both local and global executives of the sector. Turkey is the most willing and broad-visioned member of the region and can be the fundamental player by improving big data technologies in healthcare infrastructure nationwide. In conclusion, by joining MENA zone, Turkey can reflect its hidden potential and dominate the medium by the cooperation of governing policy makers and industrial sponsors eager to boost investments in this region.

References

1. https://clinicaltrials.gov/ct2/about-studies/learn#ClinicalTrials (Access Date 05.01.2021).
2. Guideline on strategies to identify and mitigate risks for first-in-human and early clinical trials with investigational medicinal products, European Medicines Agency, Committee for Medicinal Products for Human Use, EMEA/CHMP/SWP/28367/07 Rev. 1, 20 July 2017 (Access Date 05.01.2021).
3. Ertok Ö, Akbil Ş, Sakallıoğlu Y. Benefits of a clinical research strategy for Turkey, A roadmap for innovation-driven growth, IQVIA, 2020.
4. https://www.marketdataforecast.com/market-reports/mea-clinical-trials-market (Access Date 05.01.2021).
5. www.clinicaltrials.gov (Access Date 05.01.2021).
6. Ebrahim S, Bassil N. Unearthing the potential of the clinical trial market in Middle East, Turkey and Africa (Meta) Region, IQVIA, 2020.
7. Erdoğan B, Şeker Ö, Chin LV. Regulations and recruitment: Experiences in the Middle East. Journal for Clinical Studies. 2017; 9(3), 30–34.

Özgür Kasapçopur, Mehmet Yıldız, Fatih Özdener

Ethical Considerations (Clinical Research in Pediatric and Sensitive Populations)

Mankind's tendency to achieve the right, beautiful, and good that has been going on for centuries is increasing in an accelerating pace. At this point, science is the most important basis of mankind. Through science, humanity will surely reach a better and a more beautiful world. The dignity and effectiveness of scientists involved in science is revealed by the research and innovations they add to science. No scientist can be separated from manufacturing, offering new ideas and different opinions. Scientists seek truth through science, try to humanize and change life, and also produce original information. In doing all this, its main stay is honesty, and it is ethical rules that were formed over the centuries that it depends on, one of humanity's greatest assets. The word "ethics" comes from a combination of ethos and mores in ancient Greek and Latin and determine how individuals communicate with each other. From a philosophical point of view, it defines what is good for the individual and society and the duties of individuals for themselves and society. Ethical rules reveal what is good and right for mankind. Ethical rules help humanity in all areas of regulation of their lives. The main topic of this chapter is "Scientific Research Ethics."

The first studies with scientific research ethics have been the issue of the most intense violations of rights. It started after World War II. The Helsinki declaration, which was first introduced in Nuremberg courts and was first based on this data, was created in 1964 and updated for years, guiding clinical research on human beings (1). In the light of this information, "Good Clinical practices" (GCP) have been developed, which also provide guidance for clinical research (2). Evaluating clinical medical researches all over the world is based on all these regulations and rules. Clinical Research Ethical Committees (CREC) or Institutional Review Boards (IRB) have been created. Clinical medical researches to be carried out all over the world must first be approved by an independent CREC or IRB.

The CREC structure must evaluate all applications made according to the universal ethical rules. CRECs are established in every major research center, first by local governments and then by permission from the authority. Each newly established CREC should have clinicians, medical pharmacologists, medical ethics specialists, lawyers, and civilian members from various branches of expertise. All of these members must have had received GCP training. CRECs form their own "standard operational procedure" (SOP) at the first time they are created. CRECs primarily aim to protect the health, well-being, safety, dignity, and rights of volunteers who will participate in the clinical research by taking into account the scientific methods and the concerns of the community. CRECs were established in order to make scientific and ethical assessments of the rights, security, and well-being of volunteers, as well as other research-related topics and methods and documents to be used to inform volunteers and what would be taken from these people (3). Firstly, the clinical research form and all documents in the reference file are evaluated according to the data contained in Table 1.

Table 1: What points does the Clinical Research Ethical Committee evaluate in the research file?

Is the research based on a new hypothesis and scientific data?
Is the research ready to be conducted on humans?
What are the advantages and disadvantages expected from the research? Is it worth researching?
Are the volunteer's rights and well-being protected?
Is the informed volunteer consent form eligible?
Are the criteria for inclusion and non-inclusion appropriate for participation?
Is the research in line with the current legislation?
Is the international convention in line with standards and guidelines?
Is the research protocol design appropriate?
Has the phase been correctly determined?
Are there any facilities for the storage and distribution of the product?
Is the research team proper?
Do those responsible know if the place to investigate is appropriate and adequate?
Is the archive sufficient?
Is the research budget realistic and appropriate?

Clinical research can be initiated if the benefits are higher than the risks that are likely to arise from the research, and if the institution obtained permission, it will be carried out in the event of continuation of these conditions. Ethical committees are independent in terms of scientific and ethical evaluation and decision-making of clinical research applications. Members of the ethics committee must comply with the privacy policy for any information that reaches them. Members of the ethics committee begin their duties by signing the confidentiality document and contract prepared by the institution. The member of the ethics committee who has a relationship with the investigation or has a duty in the investigation cannot participate in the discussions and voting of this research in the ethics committee, and the ethics committee cannot sign its decision (4).

CRECs evaluate the analysis of the benefits, harms, and risks expected from the clinical research and whether it is based on scientific data and a new hypothesis, and the necessity of the research to be conducted primarily in the non-human experimental environment or on enough animals before the first clinical trial on humans. In addition, they assess the written information about clinical research, the method followed for obtaining voluntary consent, the adequacy of the rationale for the researches to be conducted on the disabled, children, pregnant women, puerperant women and nursing women, people in intensive care and unconscious persons, and the responsibility of the responsible investigator or investigator or sponsor in case of possible safety issues. CRECs evaluate compensation for injury or death associated with clinical research, regulations on the recruitment of volunteers to clinical research, the suitability of the research team involved according to the nature of the research, and the detailed budgeting of the study.

The ethics committee can monitor the approval areas from the applications made to it, if necessary, during the investigation and on-site. The ethics committee for clinical research informs the applicant within a maximum of 15 days from the date of application. In addition to the 15-day period determined for approval in clinical trials and non-drug clinical trials, which will be carried out with products carrying genetically modified organisms with products containing cellular therapies or gene therapy, a further 30-day period can be added. If the ethics committee requests additional information and explanation, all requests required will be forwarded to the applicant at once. The review process is halted until these information and documents are presented.

Another important point in clinical research is clinical research on children. At this point specifically, there are very different and subtle points (5, 6). It should not be forgotten that the child is not a copy of the adult. Childhood is a period that includes dynamic, variable, and different periods within it. The most important of the main principles in clinical research in children should be to prevent any harms that may occur. In researches to be carried out on children, useful and effective results should be foreseen first. Clinical investigations in children should be completed and shown to be effective on the adult as long as appropriate. Children also need effective treatment methods; it is a reality that should not be forgotten. In order to ensure the validity of the research, it is important to create the research design after consulting patients or patient representatives from the age groups (seniors or adolescents) to be included in the research. A special attention should be paid to the inclusion (and possibly detection) of subsets with specific genetic features (e.g. G6PDH deficiency) as well as age-group choices in children to be included in the study. As with adult studies, all necessary measures should be taken to avoid bias in studies with children. Uncontrolled studies to demonstrate effectiveness should, in principle, be avoided. The scope of studies with children should be as narrow as possible, but with the right statistical power, it should be sufficient to demonstrate the right necessary effectiveness. When conducting clinical researches on children, the features obtained in Table 2 should be considered.

Table 2: Points to be taken in consideration for scientific researches in children

Identification and scientific validity of the question to be answered in the research.
The reason for the research, which will be carried out with children and recommended age groups.
Proof of direct benefit to the individual or the benefit of the group.
Proficiency level of the researcher and their team responsible for the research.
Especially in the field of the implemented project, the infrastructure of the institution or research center should be qualified and experienced in pediatric research in general.
Pre-clinical safety and efficacy data (such as research brochure, current literature) which are prerequisites for pediatric clinical trials.
Clinical findings of studies with adults, if any (such as literature, research brochure).
Age-appropriate formulations of medical products.
Age-appropriate scale or measurements of endpoints (such as pain scale).
Biometric planning in connection with the design of the research and the question of the research.
Design applicability and information forms checked by the child/patient representatives.
Criteria for inclusion and exclusion in the research.

Firstly, not to harm the child should be foreseen as the main principle. Especially in blood sampling, it should be satisfied with as few samples as possible. Studies should be arranged, if appropriate, with waste such as urine, breath, or feces which can be obtained without interference. Research protocols and processes applied in adults should not be used one-on-one in children and should be reorganized. Researches should be carried out by capturing statistical significance with as few patients as possible. Placebo-controlled studies in children are very difficult to execute and are not feasible. This issue remains controversial. One of the important points in clinical researches in children is the risk assessment. One of the most important points here is that the interests of the child are always kept above the interests of science and society. This principle is the most important element in the evaluation and monitoring of risks. Risks should be seen in balance with the benefit to be provided. Risk assessment is the most important stage in the evaluation of the protocol and in the execution of the research. The risk assessment involves the evaluation of the tested product or to check, in some cases, the failure to administer effective treatment and the risks of the disease itself.

One of the most important points of clinical research in children is to receive informed consent. This is a very dynamic process with different steps. It is the most important part of the research. It is a continuous process that is taken while the child, family, and researcher are together. All the processes in the research should be laid out in detail. In particular, all of the acute conditions that may occur in chronic diseases should be explained in detail. The process of obtaining the informed consent is summarized in Table 3.

Table 3: Mandatory points in the informed consent form

The purpose, structure, and duration of the research.
Accurate disclosure of the procedures to be done within the scope of the research.
Scientific benefits expected from the study.
The difficulties and limitations that the research may cause.
Possible risks that may occur in the study.
Alternative to procedures that can harm the volunteer.
The person to be included in the study is free to participate, not to participate, and withdraw consent at any stage of the trial.
It should be made clear that not participating in the study or withdrawal would not create a physician's bias.
The consent form should be cleared of medical language as much as possible. It should be in a language that the patient can understand.

The use of placebo should be avoided as much as possible in clinical drug research in children. If it is to be used, the use of placebo and control groups should be based on an element of balance, and it must be in accordance with the conditions investigated in the study and justified scientifically. Placebo should not be used, especially if it prevents effective treatment in severe and life-threatening conditions. If the event is to be tried, the use of placebo in volunteers should be used after the active drug is provided. If a new exacerbation occurs in the use of placebo, the active drug should be started again quickly.

As a result, with the medical researches carried out with unfailing adherence to universal scientific and ethical rules, the efforts of humanity that has been going on for centuries to reach the truth and find the right information will continue with an increasing momentum and perhaps the process of humanization, not the destruction of nature, can be completed.

References

1. World Medical Association Declaration of Helsinki: Ethical principles for medical research involving human subjects. Jama. 2013;310(20):2191–4.
2. Vijayananthan A, Nawawi O. The importance of Good Clinical Practice guidelines and its role in clinical trials. Biomedical Imaging and Intervention Journal. 2008;4(1):e5–e.
3. Das NK, Sil A. Evolution of ethics in clinical research and ethics committee. Indian J Dermatol. 2017;62(4):373–9.
4. McLean SAM. What and who are clinical ethics committees for? Journal of medical ethics. 2007;33(9):497–500.
5. Ethical issues in health research in children. Paediatrics & child health. 2008;13(8):707–20.
6. Roth-Cline M, Gerson J, Bright P, Lee CS, Nelson RM. Ethical considerations in conducting pediatric research. Handb Exp Pharmacol. 2011;205:219–44.

Bilge Aydın Temiz

The Requirement and Importance of Legal Regulations in Drug Clinical Trials

The general purpose of medical science is protecting human health, treating diseases, and improving the patients' quality of life. From this point of view, medical science seems to be developing constantly. The importance of clinical trials of drugs in achieving this improvement is indisputable. However, sad events have been experienced in the history of clinical trials around the world. These experiments caused permanent injury or death of people.

In world history, clinical studies conducted without complying with medical ethics and legal rules have had serious results. Some of these events are described below.

Tuskegee Syphilis Studies (1932–1972)

It is a clinical study on syphilis conducted between 1932 and 1972 on the black male population living in Tuskegee, a residential area in Alabama, USA. Although the use of penicillin was started for the treatment of syphilis during the study period, this clinical study continued, and patients participating in the study were deliberately left untreated. The researchers continued to collect data that was important to them. During the study, many patients died, some of their spouses had syphilis, and some of their babies were born with syphilis.

The Sulfonamide Elixir Incident (1938)

Sulfonamide, which was frequently used as tablets and powder in the US in the 1930s, was put on the market by producing its solution for children's use. However, 107 children who used this solution died within 1–3 weeks due to its toxic effects. This event, which is referred to as the "Elixir Sulfanilamide Incident," is regarded as the foundation of the structure providing broad authority to the FDA in the US.

Studies of Nazi Doctors (1940–1944)

It is known that some German doctors conducted experiments on thousands of prisoners in concentration camps without their consent and without obeying any legal rule during the Second World War. These experiments, which were carried out against human dignity and without legal grounds, often ended in death.

Thalidomide Children Disaster (1950–1961)

In Europe, the nausea drug called "Thalidomide" was used to stop nausea and insomnia complaints of women during pregnancy. More than 10 thousand babies were born without arms, legs, and fingers all over the world because of this drug, which was only used to stop nausea. Although the experiments made on pregnant mice provided quite successful and safe results, the use of this drug in pregnant women resulted in the birth of thousands of impaired babies with short arms and legs, called "phocomelia," which is defined as the "congenital skeletal disorder where at least one of the arms and legs have a missing end piece."

Willowbrook School Hepatitis Study (1963–1966)

Live hepatitis virus was given to newly enrolled children to learn the natural course of hepatitis between 1963 and 1966 in the Willowbrook State School, New York, where mentally retarded children were educated. During the study period, parents who wanted to enroll their children in the school were required to give their consent for their children to be included in this study. This unethical and illegal study conducted to find an effective vaccine against hepatitis has taken its place among the tragedies in the history of medicine.

Considering these tragedies, it is obvious how vital legal regulations are in the clinical trials of drugs. Serious legal regulations are required particularly for protecting human dignity and human rights. After all, medical science and legal science are two fields that directly affect each other, and they need to be studied together. While medical science aims to protect human life and health, legal science aims to protect the fundamental rights and freedoms that people need as much as health.

In This Context, International Documents on Clinical Trials Created by the Relevant Authorities

(A) *Those with binding nature*
1. United Nations International Covenant on Civil and Political Rights (Article 7)
2. Convention on Human Rights and Biomedicine
3. European Union Directive on Clinical Drug Research

(B) *Advisory ones*
  1. Nuremberg Codex
  2. Helsinki Declaration
  3. International Guideline on Biomedicine Research in Human Subjects
  4. UNESCO Universal Declaration of Bioethics and Human Rights
  5. Guideline for Good Clinical Practice

International legal norms also have prevailing principles to protect the fundamental rights and freedoms of people participating in any clinical trial. Almost all of the abovementioned regulations cover these normative principles and regulations. In short, these are the principle of respect for autonomy, the principle of no harm, the principle of beneficence, and the principle of justice.

The principle of respect for autonomy derives from the right to make decisions about oneself. It also requires other people's respect for the decisions of an individual about themselves. From this point of view, it is compulsory to obtain the consent of the subjects who will participate in the study after informing them about the study in detail. Also, the participant has the right to leave the study at any stage without being subjected to any sanctions, even if he/she initially participates in the study of his own free will. Also, it should be ensured that his/her treatment will not be adversely affected when he/she leaves. The risk/benefit analysis should be conducted in detail before initiating the clinical trial due to **the principle of no harm**. What is important is that the expected benefit from the research should be greater than the estimated risk. As also stated by Hippocrates, the obligation of doing no harm is the basic principle of medical ethics. In this context, all measures should be taken to minimize the risks that may arise from the research, to protect the health and life of the subjects, and to minimize the troubles to be faced.

The researcher also has an obligation of doing no harm to the subject participating in the research and **conducting the research for his/her benefit**. This situation reveals the researchers' positive obligation: they should not do harm to the subject; moreover, they should conduct the research for the benefit of the subject. With **the principle of justice**, first of all, the answer to the question of who will participate in a clinical trial and who will benefit is sought. Thus, being fair and equitable to those who can participate in the study can be achieved.

Also, in case one of the subjects participating in the clinical trial is harmed, naturally, the damage must be compensated. Usually, how the damage will be compensated is clearly stated in the contracts. However, it will be possible to compensate within the general legal norms even if it is not stipulated in the contracts. As a matter of fact, any unlawful intervention to the individual's personal rights protected by the law is an illegal act, and responsibility arises due to any tort.

It is essential to protect the rights and safety of all subjects participating in the clinical trial. In this context, all the details of the study and the procedures to be performed should be communicated to the subjects ensuring that they understand all the information given. The subjects should be given enough time to decide whether to participate in the clinical trial. It should be ensured to duly receive the Informed Consent Form (ICF) from the subject. The necessary medical assistance should be provided to the subject in case of any adverse effects during the research.

The study protocol must be followed precisely so that the subjects are protected better against the risks. Relevant parties should be immediately informed of any development that may arise during the study. Undoubtedly, a clinical trial of a drug is a teamwork. All the team members participating in the study should be ensured to receive adequate training. The entire team should thoroughly understand the details of the study; also, they should know all standards on protecting the rights of subjects participating in the study in detail.

Another important issue in a clinical trial is receiving the required records, information, and documents as specified and keeping them in accordance with the legislation. The subject must be informed in detail about the study, and his/ her consent must be obtained. The research should be performed following methodological approaches in the light of scientific data; random and uncontrolled studies should be avoided. The research should not cause any unnecessary physical and mental problems in the subject.

As a result, it is really important to conduct clinical trials in a country. In fact, the statistics reveal that most of the clinical trials have been conducted in developed countries. From this point of view, there seems no reason for not conducting more clinical trials in the MENA region because of the existence of reputable health institutions and scientists.

As a matter of fact, thanks to clinical trials of drugs, patients will have the opportunity to access the drug earlier and contribute to the developments in science; also, opinion leaders and scientists will have their rightful place in the international arena. However, it should be noted again that carrying out all the studies following the provisions of the legislation and ethical rules should be the basic principle.

The clinical trial of a drug requires complying with many regulations due to their nature; therefore, it cannot be stated that making exclusive regulations only for clinical trials and improving them in the process is sufficient. Making regulations to increase the number and quality of trials in the countries will be very beneficial. For example, in practice, many problems are experienced in the insurance transactions for the clinical trials in many countries. Therefore, legal regulations are needed for insurance specific to clinical studies. Also, many regulations should be made to improve the content of the training, the working conditions, and the personal rights of the people employed in this field to ensure better training for them.

Besides, incentives should be brought up on the agenda for the clinical trials to be carried out. Due to its nature, the clinical trials also bring up many discussions along with them. For example, it is possible to come across many articles and opinions stating that the subjects participating in the study were used as guinea pigs. However, more studies should be conducted and examples of good practices (provided that personal data are protected) should be shared with the public to eliminate this perception. In fact, positive results will be obtained if everyone participating in clinical trials of drugs behave quite sensitively, ethically, and in accordance with the law and if the control mechanisms are well operated.

Finally, whether any fee is paid to subjects participating in the clinical trials of drugs should be mentioned. This is one of the most discussed topics. According to regulations in some countries, it is not possible to make any convincing incentives or financial offers to the subjects or their legal representatives to participate in or continue to research except for the coverage of the insurance. However, the costs incurred by the subject's participation in the research and the income loss of healthy subjects arising from the study are specified in the research budget and covered by this budget. It is known that the subjects get a certain amount of payment for their participation in the clinical trial in some developed countries. In my opinion, considering the actual situations and realities of certain countries, the principle of being a volunteer should be followed for a while more since the payments to subjects causes public debates. However, legal regulations will be made on these issues after a while, and a fee can be paid within the ethical limits based on the approval of the ethics committees and on the condition that it is not excessive.

To conclude, diseases exist in all environments where people live, and there is a thought that people seek a remedy in each environment where there is a disease. Throughout history, people have continually searched for new drugs and new techniques to cure existing diseases. Thanks to these efforts and scientific curiosity, human civilization and particularly the medical world have developed, and they continue to develop. Therefore, it has never been a rational approach to put barriers to the concepts of "science, clinical trial, research, experiment" and to prohibit such studies due to the possible risks that may arise in clinical trials on humans. Such studies should be supported at every stage, but medical ethics and legal rules should not be ignored. Just as it is an indisputable fact that the scientists' research and development studies should be supported, it is another undeniable fact that all kinds of studies in this field should be carried out within the framework of legal rules and should be kept under strict control by health authorities. The fields where studies directly affecting human health and life are carried out should not be left unlawful and uncontrolled.

Adv. Bilge Aydın Temiz-LLM

References

1. Medical Law, Hakan Hakeri, Seçkin Publishing House 18. Edition
2. Problems and Solutions in Clinical Trials (Questions and Answers) Prof. Dr. Işık Tuğlular-Associate Professor Uğur Öncel Türk
3. Ministry of Health Good Clinical Practice Guideline
4. Regulation on Clinical Trials
5. Helsinki Declaration
6. Convention on Human Rights and Biomedicine
7. The Universal Declaration of Human Rights, declared by the United Nations General Assembly on 10 December 1948
8. Scientific Medicine, Clinical Research Book 2014-Editors Prof. Dr. Hamdi Akan, Dr. Hilal Aybars, Nurşah Ömeroğlu Çetinkaya
9. Özlem Yenerer Çakmut, Criminal Law Examination of Consent to Medical Intervention, Istanbul 2003
10. Tuğrul Katoğlu, Council of Europe Convention on Human Rights and Biomedicine as Part of Turkish Law, AÜHFD, YIŞ 2006, VOL 55 Issue 1
11. Erşen Şen, The Crime of Experimentation on Human (TCK 90) Istanbul Bar Association Journal, Vol 79 November-December, No 2005/6
12. Yener Ünver, Experiment and Trial Crimes on Human, Health Law Symposium Symposium 1 2007

Mutlu Hayran, Deniz Yüce

Importance of Epidemiological Data

The fundamental definition of epidemiology is *"the study of the distribution and determinants of health-related states or events in specified populations, and the application of this study to control of health problems"* in the Dictionary of Epidemiology (1). During the natural evolution of this definition, epidemiology coverage has extended from the study of communicable disease epidemics to all health-related conditions. And the inclusion of clinical research into this definition yielded a new branch of study, namely *Clinical Epidemiology*.

From a semantic perspective, clinical epidemiology refers to a discipline that applies epidemiological methods in clinical research. In a broader meaning, epidemiology studies disease occurrence in human populations, whereas clinical research focuses more on predicting individual-level clinical events (2). The first use of the term "clinical epidemiology" was by John Rodman Paul. He described it as *"a marriage between quantitative concepts used by epidemiologists to study disease in populations and decision-making in the individual case which is the daily fare of clinical medicine"* (3). Applying epidemiological methods and best practices beginning from study design to reporting the outcomes during clinical research is the key to improve the quality of evidence and the inferences from sample populations by avoiding systematic errors. The products of these studies guide decision-making processes that shape clinical applications in practice.

The practical application of clinical epidemiology has also been a basis for the development of the Evidence-Based Medicine (EBM) concept (4, 5), which is a contemporary definition that adds patient care to epidemiological applications in clinical research (6). From a practical point of view, evidence-based medicine structures the most appropriate research design and analytical methods to confirm the validity of evidence from research to establish a strong basis for clinical applications (7). The level of evidence may vary, but the background for obtaining this evidence is assured when epidemiologic principles are met in clinical research.

This chapter gives a brief introduction to epidemiological study types and focuses on the importance of epidemiological data, particularly in settings with limited infrastructure and challenges concerning clinical research.

Epidemiologic Studies

Epidemiology basically evaluates the interactions between person, place, and time. From an aspect of infectious diseases, these are agent, host, and environment. These evaluations may vary based on several critical determinants like study question, hypothesis, and outcome measure, and selecting the appropriate study type is the initial step for conducting epidemiological research. As a general rule of thumb, the primary discrimination between epidemiologic study designs is an intervention that separates the *observational* and *experimental* studies (8). The observational studies may be either descriptive or analytical based on the existence of a control group or hypothesis to be tested. Descriptive studies do not include a control group or test a hypothesis (1). Analytical studies collect data in generally two or more groups of cases and compare the measures of interest between them. Still, the researcher is not involved in the assignment of subjects into the study groups. On the other hand, the researcher designates the group assignment in experimental studies. Another essential difference between the analytical study types is the direction of the temporality. If the researcher measures the outcome starting from the exposure, this is called a cohort study. Conversely, if the researcher already knows the outcome but measures the presence or absence of exposure, this is called a case/control study. If the exposure and outcome are measured simultaneously, this is called a cross-sectional study (9) (Figure 1).

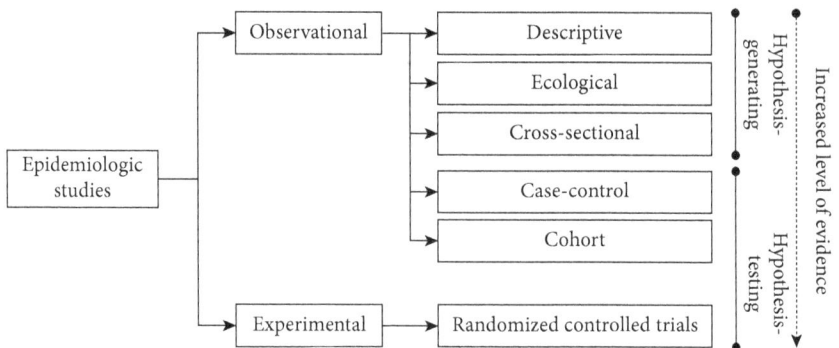

Figure 1: Epidemiologic study designs (10)

Observational Studies

When dealing with a health-related issue, the first step is to describe the situation using five critical questions – *what, who, why, when, where*. Proper answers to these questions should be concluded with an additional question – *so what* (11, 12). A good descriptive study should provide adequate information to cover these critical questions.

First question, ***what***, explicitly defines the condition of interest. This may be a disease or another health-related condition that affects individuals toward an increased health risk or benefit regarding preventive measures. In each situation, the condition of interest should be clearly defined to the target audience. The second question, ***who***, should describe the population who have this health-related condition. The characteristics of individuals like sociodemographic, economic, cultural, ethnic backgrounds, etc. can significantly affect their vulnerability or resistance against the exposure in the study. ***Why***, does not directly answer the causal factors of the outcome, but may provide some clues that can be evaluated in further methodologically more sophisticated studies. ***When***, is an important question that can give valuable hints for assessing temporality or identifying preceding risk factors that can cause the outcome. And, the last question, ***where***, is as important as the basic demographic characteristics of individuals, because geography is a well-established determinant of health since Hippocrates. If a descriptive study answers these questions in detail, then the central question raises, ***so what*** (11). This question can be considered as a valuation of the descriptive study. It answers the impact of the study regarding public health or contribution to scientific evidence. When planning the descriptive research, it may be the first question to be answered in many cases, particularly if the study is a continuum of an already established literature.

Observational studies provide valuable information for defining health-related situations if data is collected considering the key points explained above. Using the available information, researchers can define the time trends that change over decades, years, months, or even days in rapidly disseminating diseases, the demographic differences to evaluate the affected groups or the geographic areas where the condition shows specific distribution patterns. The results of the descriptive studies can provide an overall comprehension and can be presented using interpretable charts, figures, maps, or summary tables.

Typical examples of descriptive studies include case reports and case-series reports. These studies are based on the researcher's observations in one clinical case or group of subjects with similar clinical characteristics. Another type of descriptive research is ecological studies, also called correlation studies. These studies have the convenience of using already collected data from different sources, and they make assumptions based on the correlations between them. The measurements are at the population level and prone to an ecological fallacy, which means that the inferences from population-level associations may not reflect individual associations. Another descriptive study type is the cross-sectional design. Cross-sectional studies are also referred to as taking a snapshot in time (9). Since they collect data at a specific time point, the outcome measure is generally disease frequency or prevalence. But surveillance studies can also be conducted to monitor the diseases continuously if data collection continues regularly. An example of such a study is presented in Figure 2. During the COVID-19 pandemic, relevant data were collected by the World Health Organization from countries regularly, and the results were evaluated to direct the efforts to control the dissemination of the disease on local and global scales, and the burden of the pandemic was presented to the world by easily interpreted visualization methods (13).

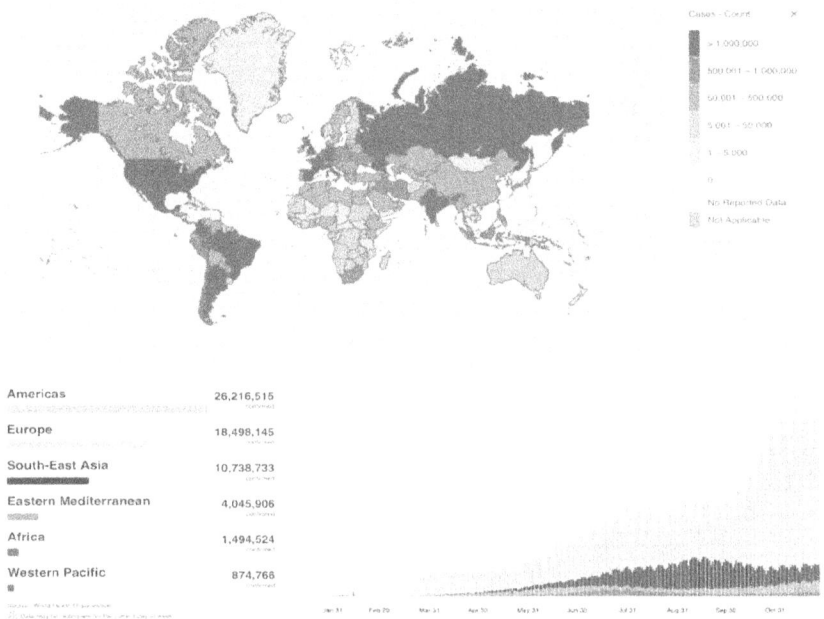

Figure 2: World Health Organization's COVID-19 surveillance data

Analytical Studies

Although they are observational, analytical studies also have the advantage of being used for hypothesis testing in addition to hypothesis-generating as in descriptive studies. The observations in descriptive studies may yield novel research questions or hypotheses that can be evaluated in further analytical studies. The main difference that makes an observational study analytical is the presence of a comparison group. Two main groups of analytical epidemiologic studies are cohort studies and case-control studies. These are nonexperimental in nature, which means that the researcher does not intervene in the study groups for one or more specific exposures. But these studies can also be considered as natural experimental studies since the exposure is present in individuals without the intervention of the study. In cohort studies, the aim is to follow up the individuals with and without the exposure and measure if disease outcome will develop or not. Cohort studies can be conducted either in prospective or retrospective fashions. Prospective cohort studies are more reliable due to the timely collection of data and having the versatility of making necessary optimizations in data collection that may emerge during the follow-up time. From this perspective, retrospective cohort studies are strictly bound with the quality of the available data and can produce reliable results if data integrity is assured. Comparing the outcome in exposed and unexposed groups gives the absolute risk attributed to the risk factor, called the relative risk (RR).

The second type of analytical design is case-control studies. This study design starts with the outcome. The researcher assigns participants into groups with (case) and without (control) the outcome measure and evaluates exposure to the risk factor in the past. These studies are more appropriate if the outcome of interest is rare or a condition that develops over a significantly longer period. Once the outcome is known, researchers collect data of exposure in the past using different data sources like personal declarations, families, relatives, hospital records, etc. As collecting data from the past is prone to information or recall bias, the data sources' quality must be ensured. Moreover, as the general population is not known in case-control studies, absolute risk attributed to the risk factor cannot be calculated. The outcome measure in these studies is the odds ratio (OR), which compares the odds of having or not having the risk factor.

Experimental Studies

The key feature of the experimental studies is the presence of an intervention. Researchers assign participants to study groups with and without intervention, generally through a randomization process. If the intervention is a therapeutic intervention in patients, then this is called a randomized controlled clinical trial, and if the intervention is a preventive measure in the general population, this is called a randomized controlled field trial. In both studies, participants are first randomized to study arms, then administered either an experimental intervention or placebo (or nonexperimental intervention), and the outcomes are measured at the end of the study period. These studies are considered the gold standard in clinical research because they avoid selection and confounding biases. Nevertheless, they are not without disadvantages, and the most important one is the generalizability to the entire population. This is also called external validity, which refers to that the study was conducted on exclusively selected participants, and the outcomes may not reflect the general population. Nevertheless, randomized controlled clinical trials have the highest level of evidence among all epidemiologic study designs.

Evidence-Based Medicine

As mentioned earlier, EBM is the junction of patient values, best clinical practices, and best available scientific evidence, which aims to aid the clinical decision-making processes in healthcare (14). The EBM is gaining more importance as the amount of scientific data accumulates rapidly and becomes more complicated in parallel to the advances in modern medical sciences. The evaluation of the quality of the data is a two-sided issue. The researchers should consider the methodologic quality of the study on one side, and readers should be able to assess the quality of evidence on the other side. At this point, having knowledge and a clear understanding of epidemiological principles is the key to achieve these targets on both sides. The EBM principally considers relating the clinical signs of the patients with the best scientific evidence to solve the questions that emerge during the clinical practice. From this point of view, the best scientific evidence is provided by randomized controlled trials (RCTs) (15). Nevertheless, many RCTs may evaluate the same or different components of the same clinical condition, and it may be difficult for practitioners to follow all recent evidence published continuously. The meta-analyses and systematic reviews can overcome this issue and provide collaborated evidence to the readers.

The levels of evidence vary according to the study type and were first described by the Canadian Task Force on the Periodic Health Examination in 1979 (16). The aim of this original classification of the level of evidence was to base the recommendations on periodic health exams on the evidence in the available literature data. This classification was then revised by Sackett in 1989 (17). The most recent classification of the levels of evidence was developed by the Oxford Center for Evidence-Based Medicine in 2009 (18). The original and the revised versions of the classification of the level of evidence is presented in Table 1. Accordingly, the levels of evidence range from the highest level obtained by systematic reviews of RCTs to the lowest level of evidence from expert opinions or bench studies.

Table 1: Classifications of the levels of evidence

Classification	Level	Type of evidence
Canadian Task Force on the Periodic Health Examination's classification (16)		
	I	At least 1 RCT with proper randomization
	II.1	Well-designed cohort or case-control study
	II.2	Time series comparisons or dramatic results from uncontrolled studies
	III	Expert opinions
Sackett's classification (17)		
	I	Large RCTs with clear cut results
	II	Small RCTs with unclear results
	III	Cohort and case-control studies
	IV	Historical cohort or case-control studies
	V	Case series, studies with no controls
OCEBM's classification (18)		
	1a	SR (with homogeneity) of RCTs
	1b	Individual RCT (with narrow Confidence Interval)
	1c	All or none
	2a	SR (with homogeneity) of cohort studies
	2b	Individual cohort study (including low-quality RCT, e.g., <80 % follow-up)
	2c	"Outcomes" Research; Ecological studies
	3a	SR (with homogeneity) of case-control studies
	3b	Individual Case-Control Study
	4	Case-series (and poor-quality cohort and case-control studies)
	5	Expert opinion without explicit critical appraisal, or based on physiology, bench research, or "first principles"

RCT: *Randomized controlled trial,* **SR:** *Systematic review*

Epidemiologic Data to Support Clinical Research

Epidemiologic data refers to accumulated information gathered from various nonexperimental observations (19). In some cases, this data may be the only source of information for answering the clinical questions due to the lack of clinical trials, which is a general concern for all medical specialties. Clinicians generally seek evidence for clinical interventions, and ignoring the epidemiologic data in the absence of an RCT relevant to the intervention should leave the practitioners unanswered. The already present results of observational studies may provide some clues about the question of interest, or researchers may design appropriate cohort or case-control studies to find answers to their questions when an RCT is not available to conduct (20). In each situation, researchers or practitioners should have a basic foundation of epidemiological principles about research designs to avoid misinterpretations of the information or possible biases associated with the relevant study design.

Clinical decision-making primarily relies on evidence from clinical trials. The main difference between epidemiologic and clinical data is the target population of the studies that they are derived from. As mentioned above, epidemiologic studies focus on the health-related factors at the population level despite the clinical studies focusing on the individual patient level (21). The gold standard for evaluating the consequences of therapeutic interventions is RCTs. The evidence-based decision-making is primarily formed on the foundation of the RCTs, which can provide both efficacy and safety data associated with the relevant intervention (22). Nevertheless, these studies are prone to several challenges even if they follow the best practice guidelines. For evaluating the supportive role of epidemiologic data in clinical research, the general challenges of clinical studies must be enlightened first.

Challenges in Clinical Studies

The most critical step for designing a clinical study is identifying the study question, which can be a significant barrier confronting the researchers if not structured appropriately. This means that the rationale of the study question has to be robust regarding both epidemiological measures as well as its clinical basis. For instance, let us suppose that the research hypotheses our studies are designed to test throughout our career is actually "true" 10 % of the time. This also means that if you perform 1000 such clinical trials, 100 of the null hypotheses must be rejected to identify the "truth" in real life situation. Considering that the trials are conducted mostly with the accepted Type-II error of 20 %, the studies that will give "true positive" results is only 80. On the other hand, the Type-I error level is 5 %, so 45 studies will provide "false positive" results from the remaining 900, which actually should have accepted the null hypothesis. Consequently, the total number of studies with a positive result is 125, but only 80 are methodologically true. This will give us a 36 % (45/125) *False Discovery Rate (FDR)*, meaning that the ideas that we test in our studies are only 10 % true, slightly over one-third of our studies will incorrectly find a positive result. If we formulate our study questions better, say our hypotheses to be true 40 % of the time, then the FDR will be as low as 8.6 % (Figure 3). This shows the importance of having proper background information and adequate experience to form a valid rationale in order to set up clinical studies asking correct questions and producing valid results.

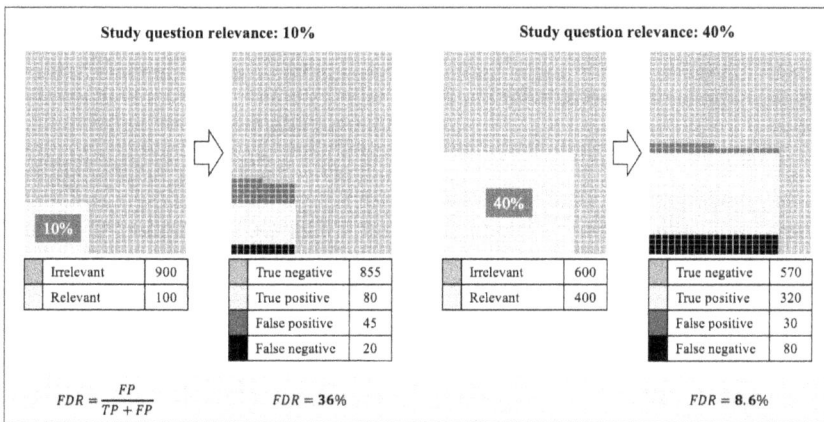

Figure 3: False discovery rates based on the relevance of the study question

Besides the methodological and clinical adequacy of the study question, it has to be also appropriate with the ethical considerations and must be relevant to the priorities of the population. This latter is particularly important because countless clinical questions remain to be answered in the era of knowledge explosion in medical sciences, but the resources are not expanding rapidly (23).

Another challenge is patient enrollment, which is closely associated with access to healthcare and coverage area of the relevant institution in specified geography or population. This directly affects the size of the target population eligible for the study. Then, the cultural factors play a significant role in the apprehension of being recruited to a clinical trial, which is also a considerable challenge for obtaining informed consent from the patients. This also includes the acceptance of randomization and subsequent adherence to assigned treatment (24–26).

Apart from recruitment factors, the human resources needed to conduct an RCT is another challenge (27). The expertise and competency of the physicians, the lack of knowledge about methodologies and conducting of clinical studies, and inadequate attention in reporting of the trials are among the most important challenges associated with human resources (28, 29). Other major barriers to conduct clinical trials are related to inadequate funding, excess regulations and monitoring, and lack of transparency at every stage of the research (30).

The Middle East and North Africa (MENA) region is seen as an opportunity for clinical trials with its large population, which is approximately more than 450 million (31), and there is a large demand for medications due to high population growth, increased life expectancy, and consequent health problems. When considered from a public health perspective, conducting clinical trials in this region is also an opportunity for the healthcare systems to access advanced therapies on a continuum to the relevant patient populations. The region attracts the pharmaceutical industry with its favorable properties, which were reported as the compliance of regulatory mechanisms with International Conference on Harmonization-Good Clinical Practices (ICH-GCP) standards, cultural factors such as trust-based relation with doctors that motivate patients to participate in clinical research, presence of well-educated and experienced clinical investigators, international affiliations of academic centers with research facilities primarily in the USA, high prevalence of chronic diseases, and comparatively lower costs of treatments (32). Besides these favorable properties, this region also has several challenges for conducting clinical trials.

From a starting point, the legal regulations are the first and sometimes the primary speed-limiting step to initiate a clinical trial. Each country in the MENA region has specific local rules. For example, in Egypt, a sequential approval procedure involving the central regulatory department, local ethical approval, and overall approval by the ministry of health is needed to initiate a trial (33). In Lebanon, the ministry of health only controls the importation of the investigational product, and the institutional review boards are responsible for the rest of the procedures (32). In Jordan, the clinical studies division of the independent regulatory agency, the Jordan Food and Drug Administration, controls the approval and initiation procedures for clinical trials in a relatively short time (34). The examples may vary but show the heterogeneity of the regulatory processes, which limits the sponsors shift the resources rapidly or comply with the changing regulations between countries.

Once the regulatory approvals are obtained, the next round of challenges is faced in the study sites. These challenges may include several components, such as lower rates of involvement of physicians in clinical trials, lack of trained personnel, infrastructural incompetence of the study sites, etc. The low number of physicians involved in clinical research is mainly related to the lack of knowledge about clinical trials. Previous reports stressed the importance of incorporating education on clinical trials and research design and methodology in the curricula of medical faculties, postgraduate programs, and continuing medical education training in the MENA region (35). The increased number of educated staff in clinical trials will be the primary driver for improving the standards of clinical research in the region.

The next challenge for clinical trials in the MENA region is the oversight of the clinical trials regarding ethical considerations. The main focus of problems associated with the ethical considerations in MENA is the lack of national guidelines in the region (36). Moreover, even if the local regulations are present, each country's diverse cultural characteristics in the region make competence with the ethical standards challenging (32). Nevertheless, the sponsors have to be entirely sure about the fulfillment of requirements. The study has to be conducted following the study protocol, GCP principles, standard operating procedures and reported in compliance with the established standards. The most practical way for following the trial from these aspects is working with a contract research organization (CRO), but sponsors generally have to perform regular and frequent site visits to monitor the trial progress in MENA countries (35). This increases the costs and may demotivate sponsors for conducting trials in countries with low commitment to internationally recognized ethical principles.

Apart from MENA's clinical or scientific challenges, there are also several societal challenges specific to the region. One of the most significant of them is the active conflicts in the Middle East and Gulf region. There is a considerable refugee crisis, very high numbers of displaced individuals, significant barriers to healthcare access, distinct patterns of communicable and chronic disorders, limited infrastructural capabilities of healthcare systems, problems in transportation of investigational products, etc. These all make the MENA disadvantageous for the industry to conduct more clinical research in the region (34).

These challenges may vary from one country to another, and not every institution or clinical setting may face these challenges (37). These obstacles are more prominent in countries with limited resources and mainly include ethical, organizational, regulatory, cultural, or infrastructural barriers (38). The limited resources should not be confused with the development status of the countries. In general, barriers in clinical trials are not associated with the countries' development status. Even developed countries face it due to the limited resources despite the high demand for clinical trials for the pending questions. For example, today, only about one-third of all clinical trials worldwide are conducting in the United

States, which was about 85 % in the 1990s, and about 60 % of the participants of clinical trials are out of the United States (39). Lower costs, potentially larger target populations with treatment-naïve patients, relatively faster recruitment courses, and less extensive regulations made clinical trials shift from developed countries to middle-income countries (40, 41). Seeking suitable regions to conduct these trials may partly relieve the obstacles, but the challenges remain at varying degrees for every research setting. Different approaches may be developed to overcome the limitations, and using epidemiologic data can aid the efforts.

Importance of Epidemiologic Data

Although conducting clinical research is challenging, the number of clinical trials is continuously growing each year (39). But not all clinical trials are RCTs, and as of the end of November 2020, approximately 21 % of 359,000 registered trials in ClinicaTrials.gov database are observational epidemiologic studies (39). The epidemiologic data provided by those studies can direct the efforts for further studies with advanced methodologies. Moreover, using epidemiologic data from observational studies may suggest specific solutions to overcome the challenges in clinical trials.

First of all, observational studies have a weaker level of evidence, and they must not be regarded as an alternative or a substitute to RCTs. Nevertheless, costs and the need for higher resources may force researchers to conduct observational studies, particularly in low-resource settings. A well-designed observational study with appropriate methodology may answer the clinical questions to some extent. There is a tendency between observational and randomized trials to correlate with the consequences of the interventions, but the treatment effects are not correlated as much, and the results should be interpreted cautiously since they may under- or overestimate the impact of intervention or exposures (42). One major advantage of observational studies over RCTs is evaluating rare diseases or treatment effects, which should be too costly and time consuming to measure (43). A case-control or cohort study may elucidate the rare outcome of interest less expensively or rapidly than an RCT. The observational studies may even have a significant role in drug development in rare diseases, which was supported by the US Food and Drug Administration (FDA) in the guidance document promoting the natural history studies to be used for this purpose (44).

Epidemiologic data can also provide valuable information about the study populations to be used in further trials. The participants' baseline characteristics, incidence and prevalence of the diseases or exposures, variances of the outcome parameters, presence and extent of the confounding parameters, etc. are essential for planning new studies. The information gathered through these studies reflects the "real world" information, which realistically describes the situation in the population. Facts, figures, and inferences from these studies are used for sample size calculations, study design, identification of confounding factors, forming study groups, determining possible sources of bias, etc. in further studies (45).

Baseline epidemiologic data can also quantify the public health impacts of various alternative study questions to identify the most appropriate ones to allocate limited resources. This can be achieved by modeling studies, forecasts and projections, and modern approaches like machine learning algorithms – all fed by the high-quality epidemiologic data accumulated in primarily observational studies (46).

One critical situation that increases the importance of epidemiologic data is the advances in computational sciences and technologies (47). In the era of the internet and big data, limitations to access the information have been abandoned, and massive data became available for evaluation. Of course, the primary aims of those databases are reaching patient data quickly rather than research purposes. But, when the essential requirements like regulatory permissions or ethical approvals are obtained, the electronic medical records, diagnostic images, biobank data, genome sequencing information, etc. are all ready for the researchers for conducting observational studies and gaining in-depth epidemiological evidence from a large data pool. These studies may reach the areas that are difficult or impossible to be evaluated by an RCT or may even prove causal relationships without a need for an RCT. Nevertheless, the possible causal mechanism proposed by analyses on data sources instead of an RCT should be confirmed only after extensive evaluation (48). Additionally, the FDR explained above should always be kept in mind when making analyses and inferences using the accumulated data. Every researcher should recognize the *garbage in – garbage out* rule when evaluating the outcomes and assumptions from these analyses.

Another important use of information from previous studies is the utilization of historical data for new RCTs. Today, there is an abundant amount of participant data from the previous clinical trials. If the fundamental differences between the new intervention and past control groups that may cause significant biases in primary comparisons are eliminated, historical data would be an appealing wealth for the further planned RCTs (49). This rich resource is also accepted by the regulatory authorities of the FDA and European Medicines Agency (EMA) (50).

Health economics is another field of study that aims to improve healthcare quality, which can also enhance the field of clinical research when used along with the epidemiological data. Health economics is defined as the science of applying economic theories to understand better and propose solutions for the challenges faced during the promotion of health for all (51). In the MENA region, the applications of the Millennium Development Goals and Sustainable Development Goals of the United Nations have contributed significantly to the improvement of the health status, which consequently increased the importance of value-based health policies and the financing of healthcare services in the region (52). In today's medicine, the economic evaluation of an intervention is also wondered as well as the clinical outcomes by regulatory authorities, researchers, healthcare providers, and physicians. The economic data can be obtained from various sources like social security or reimbursement systems, but one frequently used method is collecting data related to costs together with the clinical data in a trial (53). Utilizing such a technique can provide direct costs associated with the clinical efficacy and safety and may provide more robust inferences about the cost-effectiveness of the intervention than the analyses based on indirect data sources. But, regardless of the source of the data, evaluating the economic outcomes of the clinical interventions from multiple aspects like direct and indirect cost, cost-efficiency, disability and quality-adjusted life-years gained (DALYs and QALYs), etc., should always be evaluated in depth by the decision-makers and researchers in clinical trials. Nevertheless, there is a lack of data for economic modeling in the MENA region. There are efforts to establish an infrastructure to access the economic data of healthcare interventions, of which one example is the collaboration of the Centre for Clinical Research and Health Outcomes, GlobeMed, and Higher Institute of Public Health of Saint-Joseph University of Beirut, who came together to establish a data warehouse including the real-world evidence about the treatment of patients (54). Using health economics analyses' outcomes will contribute significantly to allocating and utilizing the limited resources to the most effective treatment and service in the region.

When the limited resources and the significant challenges for conducting clinical research are considered, enhancing the environment for epidemiological studies emerges both as a motivating factor for the researchers and improving the quality of epidemiological data in the region. Being a part of multinational cooperation or workgroup is a practical solution for conducting such a study – for example, the Safe Implementation of Treatments in Stroke (SITS)-MENA network, a prospective observational study conducted between

2014 and 2016 to compare stroke patients' characteristics in the MENA region with the non-MENA patients in the SITS international registry. This study's outcomes provided valuable information about the comparative epidemiological characteristics of stroke patients in the region and high-quality validated epidemiological data to be used in further evaluations by the health authorities and governments of MENA countries (55). Another similar study was the MORE-RAS registry conducted in the MENA countries to evaluate the RAS mutation testing practices and the epidemiological features of the newly diagnosed metastatic colorectal cancer patients. This study also provided valuable insights into the distinct genetic characteristics of the disease in the region, which showed that the dominance of wild-type RAS differs from the mutational patterns in Western countries (56). Such registries are needed in the region since many diseases' epidemiological characteristics are considerably different from the westernized or developed countries. The lifestyle factors, genetic differences, and cultural features like consanguineous marriages, the shared environmental attributes in the region, etc. emphasize the importance of registries for accumulating the epidemiological data. In the lack of such reliable data sources, estimates based on the local or small studies may be biased to reflect the actual condition. For example, dementia was reported in the literature to be epidemic or has a significant risk in the MENA, which is logically irrelevant when the region's young population is considered. A well-designed epidemiological study utilizing appropriate methods revealed that the conclusions about dementia in MENA were not correct, and the risk is not widespread in the region, as suggested (57). This last study is a good example of methodological studies that can also provide a considerable contribution to the literature when conducted appropriately.

Conclusion

The advances in medical sciences are closely bound with clinical research and strictly regulated by the regulatory rules and authorities to protect both the researcher and the participants. The need for developing new therapeutic interventions for uninvestigated clinical conditions is growing, which makes clinical trials more competitive, given limited resources. For the clinical conditions lacking RCTs, which is the foundation for the EBM, using already available epidemiologic data from various types of research designs may be a solution for answering the clinical questions, generating hypotheses, or designing the most optimal randomized controlled clinical research.

References

1. Last JM, International Epidemiological Association. A dictionary of epidemiology. 4th ed. New York: Oxford University Press; 2001. xx, 196 p.

2. Friedman GD. Primer of epidemiology. 5th ed. New York: McGraw-Hill, Medical Pub. Division; 2004. x, 401 p.

3. Paul JR. Clinical epidemiology. Journal of Clinical Investigation. 1938;17(5):539–41.

4. Anderson GM, Bronskill SE, Mustard CA, Culyer A, Alter DA, Manuel DG. Both clinical epidemiology and population health perspectives can define the role of health care in reducing health disparities. J Clin Epidemiol. 2005;58(8):757–62.

5. Braude HD. Clinical intuition versus statistics: different modes of tacit knowledge in clinical epidemiology and evidence-based medicine. Theor Med Bioeth. 2009;30(3):181–98.

6. Fletcher RH, Fletcher SW, Fletcher GS. Clinical epidemiology: the essentials. 5th ed. Philadelphia: Wolters Kluwer/Lippincott Williams & Wilkins Health; 2014. 253 p.

7. Straus S, Glasziou P, Richardson WS, Haynes RB. Evidence-based medicine: how to practice and teach EBM. 5th ed. China: Elsevier; 2019.

8. National Institutes of Health. Learn About Clinical Studies 2019 [Nov. 11, 2020]. Available from: https://www.clinicaltrials.gov/ct2/about-studies/learn.

9. Hartung DM, Touchette D. Overview of clinical research design. Am J Health Syst Pharm. 2009;66(4):398–408.

10. Elmore JG, Wild DMG, Nelson HD, Katz DL. Jekel's epidemiology, biostatistics, preventive medicine, and public health. Fifth ed. Philadelphia: Elsevier; 2020.

11. Chapman PM, Guerra LM. The "So What?" factor. Marine Pollution Bulletin. 2005;50(12):1457–8.

12. Schulz KF, Grimes DA, Horton RC. Essential concepts in clinical research: randomised controlled trials and observational epidemiology. Second ed. Edinburgh: Elsevier; 2019. x, 256 p.

13. World Health Organization. WHO Coronavirus Disease (COVID-19) Dashboard 2020 [Nov. 29, 2020]. Available from: https://covid19.who.int.

14. Masic I, Miokovic M, Muhamedagic B. Evidence based medicine – new approaches and challenges. Acta Inform Med. 2008;16(4):219–25.

15. Sackett DL, Rosenberg WM, Gray JA, Haynes RB, Richardson WS. Evidence based medicine: what it is and what it isn't. BMJ. 1996;312(7023):71–2.

16. The periodic health examination. Canadian Task Force on the Periodic Health Examination. Can Med Assoc J. 1979;121(9):1193–254.

17. Sackett DL. Rules of evidence and clinical recommendations on the use of antithrombotic agents. Chest. 1989;95(2 Suppl):2S–4S.

18. Howick J, Chalmers I, Glasziou P, Greenhalgh T, Heneghan C, Liberati A, et al. The 2011 Oxford CEBM Evidence Levels of Evidence (Introductory Document) 2011 [Nov. 15, 2020]. Available from: https://www.cebm. ox.ac.uk/resources/levels-of-evidence/levels-of-evidence-introductory-document.

19. Ni D, Jin L, Tu W. Response to early warning signals. Early warning for infectious disease outbreak 2017. London, Elsevier/Academic Press an imprint of Elsevier, pp. 75–98.

20. Concato J. Observational versus experimental studies: what's the evidence for a hierarchy? NeuroRx. 2004;1(3):341–7.

21. Hannaford PC, Webb AM. Evidence-guided prescribing of combined oral contraceptives: consensus statement. An International Workshop at Mottram Hall, Wilmslow, U.K., March, 1996. Contraception. 1996;54(3):125–9.

22. Mbuagbaw L, Thabane L, Ongolo-Zogo P, Lang T. The challenges and opportunities of conducting a clinical trial in a low resource setting: the case of the Cameroon mobile phone SMS (CAMPS) trial, an investigator initiated trial. Trials. 2011;12:145.

23. Institute of Medicine (US). Forum on Drug Discovery, Development, and Translation. Transforming Clinical Research in the United States: Challenges and Opportunities: Workshop Summary. Washington (DC): National Academies Press (US); 2010. 3, Challenges in Clinical Research. [Nov. 20, 2020]. Available from: https://www.ncbi.nlm.nih.gov/books/NBK50888/.

24. Borno H, Siegel A, Ryan C. The problem of representativeness of clinical trial participants: understanding the role of hidden costs. J Health Serv Res Policy. 2016;21(3):145–6.

25. Gupta YK, Pradhan AK, Goyal A, Mohan P. Compensation for clinical trial-related injury and death in India: challenges and the way forward. Drug Saf. 2014;37(12):995–1002.

26. Spaar A, Frey M, Turk A, Karrer W, Puhan MA. Recruitment barriers in a randomized controlled trial from the physicians' perspective: a postal survey. BMC Med Res Methodol. 2009;9:14.

27. Alemayehu C, Mitchell G, Nikles J. Barriers for conducting clinical trials in developing countries- a systematic review. Int J Equity Health. 2018;17(1):37.

28. White L, Ortiz Z, Cuervo LG, Reveiz L. Clinical trial regulation in Argentina: overview and analysis of regulatory framework, use of existing tools, and researchers' perspectives to identify potential barriers. Rev Panam Salud Publica. 2011;30(5):445–52.

29. Schulz KF, Grimes DA. Blinding in randomised trials: hiding who got what. Lancet. 2002;359(9307):696–700.

30. Djurisic S, Rath A, Gaber S, Garattini S, Bertele V, Ngwabyt SN, et al. Barriers to the conduct of randomised clinical trials within all disease areas. Trials. 2017;18(1):360.

31. The World Bank. Middle East & North Africa 2020 [15 Dec. 2020]. Available from: https://data.worldbank.org/country/ZQ.

32. Yoruk S, Tetik E. Challenges and opportunities for clinical research in the Middle East. Applied Clinical Research, Clinical Trials and Regulatory Affairs. 2014;1(2):83–7.

33. Felaefel M. Conducting clinical studies in Egypt. Journal for Clinical Studies. 2016;7(6):24.

34. Arouri A, Al-Mahrouq S, Al-Ghazawi M, Russmann D. The evolving clinical research environment in Jordan. Regulatory Rapporteur. 2015;12(4):16–21.

35. Nair SC, Ibrahim H, Celentano DD. Clinical trials in the Middle East and North Africa (MENA) Region: Grandstanding or Grandeur? Contemporary Clinical Trials. 2013;36(2):704–10.

36. Sleem H, El-Kamary SS, Silverman HJ. Identifying structures, processes, resources and needs of research ethics committees in Egypt. BMC Med Ethics. 2010;11:12.

37. Jacobs JP, St Louis JD, Scholl FG. Commentary: humanitarian outreach-providing resources and measuring quality. J Thorac Cardiovasc Surg. 2020;159(3):1000–1.

38. Dilts DM, Sandler AB. Invisible barriers to clinical trials: the impact of structural, infrastructural, and procedural barriers to opening oncology clinical trials. J Clin Oncol. 2006;24(28):4545–52.

39. National Institutes of Health. Trends, Charts, and Maps 2020 [Nov. 27, 2020]. Available from: https://www.clinicaltrials.gov/ct2/resources/trends.

40. Devasenapathy N, Singh K, Prabhakaran D. Conduct of clinical trials in developing countries: a perspective. Curr Opin Cardiol. 2009;24(4):295–300.

41. Hayasaka E. Approaches vary for clinical trials in developing countries. J Natl Cancer Inst. 2005;97(19):1401–3.

42. Ioannidis JP, Haidich AB, Pappa M, Pantazis N, Kokori SI, Tektonidou MG, et al. Comparison of evidence of treatment effects in randomized and nonrandomized studies. JAMA. 2001;286(7):821–30.

43. Gagne JJ, Thompson L, O'Keefe K, Kesselheim AS. Innovative research methods for studying treatments for rare diseases: methodological review. BMJ. 2014;349:g6802.

44. Food and Drug Administration. Rare Diseases: Natural History Studies for Drug Development Guidance for Industry 2019 [01 Dec. 2020]. Available from: https://www.fda.gov/regulatory-information/search-fda-guidance-documents/rare-diseases-natural-history-studies-drug-development.

45. Manack A, Turkel CC, Kaplowitz H. Role of epidemiological data within the drug development lifecycle: A chronic migraine case study. Epidemiology - Current Perspectives on Research and Practice 2012.

46. Fairchild G, Tasseff B, Khalsa H, Generous N, Daughton AR, Velappan N, et al. Epidemiological data challenges: planning for a more robust future through data standards. Front Public Health. 2018;6:336.

47. Protti D. Commentary: the benefits and impacts of the MOE/MAR implementation: a quantitative approach. Healthcare Quarterly. 2006;10(sp):83

48. Frakt AB, Pizer SD. The promise and perils of big data in healthcare. Am J Manag Care. 2016;22(2):98–9.

49. Lim J, Wang L, Best N, Liu J, Yuan J, Yong F, et al. Reducing patient burden in clinical trials through the use of historical controls: appropriate selection of historical data to minimize risk of bias. Ther Innov Regul Sci. 2020;54(4):850–60.

50. Lim J, Walley R, Yuan J, Liu J, Dabral A, Best N, et al. Minimizing patient burden through the use of historical subject-level data in innovative confirmatory clinical trials: review of methods and opportunities. Ther Innov Regul Sci. 2018;52(5):546–59.

51. Johns Hopkins Bloomberg School of Public Health. What is Health Economics? 2020 [18 Dec. 2020].

52. Zrubka Z, Rashdan O, Gulácsi L. Health Economic Publications from the Middle East and North Africa Region: a scoping review of the volume and methods of research. Global Journal on Quality and Safety in Healthcare. 2020;3(2):44–54.

53. O'Sullivan AK, Thompson D, Drummond MF. Collection of health-economic data alongside clinical trials: is there a future for piggyback evaluations? Value Health. 2005;8(1):67–79.

54. Maskineh C, Becker RV, Kosremelli Asmar M, Bekhazi H, Sleilaty G. Php265 – landscape assessment of a Mena healthcare database for use in health economics modeling. Value in Health. 2018;21:S194–S5.

55. Rukn SA, Mazya MV, Hentati F, Sassi SB, Nabli F, Said Z, et al. Stroke in the Middle-East and North Africa: A 2-year prospective observational study of stroke characteristics in the region—Results from the Safe Implementation of Treatments in Stroke (SITS)–Middle-East and North African (MENA). International Journal of Stroke. 2019;14(7):715–22.

56. Oukkal M, Bouzid K, Bounedjar A, Alnajar A, Taleb FA, Alsharm A, et al. Middle East & North Africa registry to characterize RAS mutation status and tumour specifications in recently diagnosed patients with metastatic colorectal cancer (MORE-RAS Study). Annals of Oncology. 2019;30, Supplement 5, V246,

57. Bamimore MA, Zaid A, Banerjee Y, Al-Sarraf A, Abifadel M, Seidah NG, et al. Familial hypercholesterolemia mutations in the Middle Eastern and North African region: a need for a national registry. Journal of Clinical Lipidology. 2015;9(2):187–94.

Barış Erdoğan, Le Vin Chin

Clinical Research and Healthcare Digitalization in the Middle East and Turkey

Introduction

Home to 449 million people (1) or 5.8 % of the world's population, the countries of the Middle East form a small but significant patient cluster, not yet fully explored for the purposes of clinical research. The region actually runs 6.3 % of the trials registered on clinicaltrials.gov, but Israel, which has a developed clinical infrastructure, takes a large proportion of this. Taking out Israel, the rest of the Middle East performs 4.4 % of the trials, despite having a population which is 5.6 % of the world's (2). Of the remaining countries, the standout star, with a high number of trials and a high level of trials per capita, is Turkey. Table 1 shows the relevant numbers for each country, as well as for the region as a whole.

	Pop '000 (UN, 2019)(1)		#open trials (clinicaltrials.gov, 2021)(2)		Trials per capita	Trial share vs population share	Pharmaceuticals market (3)(4)	
WORLD	**7 794 799**		**94 527**				**1 200**	
Bahrain	1 702	0.02%						
Cyprus	1 207	0.02%	37	0.04%	3.07%	253%		
Egypt	102 334	1.31%	1 623	1.72%	1.59%	131%		
Iran (Islamic Republic of)	83 993	1.08%	110	0.12%	0.13%	11%		
Iraq	40 223	0.52%	14	0.01%	0.03%	3%		
Israel	8 656	0.11%	1 806	1.91%	20.86%	1720%		
Jordan	10 203	0.13%	95	0.10%	0.93%	77%		
Kuwait	4 271	0.05%	33	0.03%	0.77%	64%		
Lebanon	6 825	0.09%	169	0.18%	2.48%	204%		
Oman	5 107	0.07%	19	0.02%	0.37%	31%		
Qatar	2 881	0.04%	52	0.06%	1.80%	149%		
Saudi Arabia	34 814	0.45%	236	0.25%	0.68%	56%		
State of Palestine	5 101	0.07%						
Syrian Arab Republic	17 501	0.22%	10	0.01%	0.06%	5%		
Turkey	84 339	1.08%	1 691	1.79%	2.01%	165%		
United Arab Emirates	9 890	0.13%	85	0.09%	0.86%	71%		
Yemen	29 826	0.38%		0.00%	0.00%	0%		
Middle East	**448 873**	**5.8%**	**5 980**	**6.3%**			**23**	**1.9%**
Middle East minus Israel	**440 217**	**5.6%**	**4 174**	**4.4%**				

Table 1: Population, clinical trials and pharma size by countries in the Middle East.

It should be noted that these statistics only reflect trials which are reported on clinicaltrials.gov. In an earlier article, the authors' own research found that Iran, for example, was then running up to 27,519 trials, reported in the country's own registries, and run as investigator-initiated trials (5).

The Situation in the Middle East

The Growth of the Pharma Market in the Middle East

The global pharmaceuticals market is USD 1.2 trillion in size and is projected to grow to USD 1.5 trillion by 2021 (3). Of that amount, USD 26 billion is projected to be spent in the Middle East in 2017. This is less than 2 % of the total, but the Middle East share is growing at 12–14 %, one of the highest growth rates in the world (4).

In the Middle East, growth is driven by a number of factors. First, population growth has led to an increasing number of people requiring medical treatments. The area reportedly also has a high prevalence for some rare and genetic diseases, with an estimated more than 2 million people in the Middle East suffering from a rare disease (4).

Second, the high rate of economic growth has increased access to better healthcare, which has a number of consequences. Better healthcare in itself costs money, but the health benefits are improved mortality rates and longer life expectancy, which means people have more years of treatment and drug consumption. Longer life expectancy also leads to higher incidence of lifestyle diseases, for example, those associated with smoking and alcohol. Obesity, diabetes, and cardiovascular disease are on the rise, and six countries of the Middle East are among the top 10 globally in terms of prevalence of Type-2 diabetes (6).

Increased affluence also creates a more selective, health-conscious, and treatment-aware population, with sophisticated healthcare needs. The Middle East shows a marked predilection for innovative treatments. One report cites: "… a strong share of spend on the modern insulins, and the newer innovative classes of pre-insulin diabetes treatments, the DPP-IVs and the GLP-1s. In Kuwait, spend on innovative treatments accounts for 73 % of all diabetes IMS audited diabetes spend; in the UAE this is 68 %" (7).

Governments across the region encourage strong healthcare programs, backed up by reimbursement for rare disease treatments (4). Improvement of infrastructure increases the patient base by improving diagnosis rates, in turn. A combination of weaker IP protection and an encouragement of the development of local industry has gone hand in hand with a push for affordable, lower-priced medication, meaning that generics will be a major market driver (and that market growth will come from volume growth) (8).

Drivers for Clinical Research in the Middle East

There are clear, high expectations for the growth in clinical trials in the Middle East. Quintiles (now IQVIA) has estimated a market of about USD 1 billion by 2022 in the whole MENA region (9). This growth will be driven by many factors.

First, the region has a high and growing population. MENA had the highest rate of population growth in the world in the twentieth century, and the region is projected to increase by a further 87 % again between 2001 and 2050 (10).

Both the growth of the population and the growth of the pharma market are drivers for the growth of clinical research in the region. With the growth of pharma comes the increased relevance of drugs developed for local genotypes, growth in local manufacture, and the efficiency savings of early regulatory approval.

As we have mentioned, the Middle East has a high incidence of some rare diseases. According to the Center of Arab Genomic Studies (CAGS), there are 774 genetic disorders caused mainly by recessive genes, possibly as a result of a high rate of consanguineous marriages (4, 9). These diseases include diabetes mellitus (for which people in MENA exhibit the second highest prevalence after the North America and Caribbean region) (11), and orphan diseases such as Gaucher's disease, Fabry disease, Behçet's disease, thalassemia, and sickle cell anemia. The region also has high levels of hepatitis, chronic respiratory diseases such as asthma, cancer, cardiovascular disease, obesity, and psychiatric diseases (9, 12, 13). Studies have shown that 3 % of pregnancies result in a child with a significant genetic disease (13). As a result, governments in the Gulf region reimburse for rare diseases (4).

Running clinical trials in countries with high prevalence of certain diseases also allows a head start in regulatory registration: Trial results can be designed for relevance to local regulations. Marketing authorization approvals and subsequent reimbursement gain extra leverage when clinical research is done on a country's own population.

Looking at patients, there is a high willingness to join trials in the Middle East. Quintiles (now IQVIA) research shows that "data collected on patient recruitment–related site productivity – defined as the average number of patients recruited per site in a country – indicated that MENA, in terms of patients recruited per site, is more productive than the US. In fact, some parts of MENA proved incredibly productive: for example, the combination of Egypt, Jordan,

Lebanon and Syria produced a patient recruitment–related site productivity of 475 per cent of US levels." (9)

At the same time, the region has developed a very good infrastructure to run international clinical trials. There has been a rapid adoption of a high level of technology, for example, Turkey's new digitized submission process, which promises first feedback within 48 hours, making some medical facilities in the region world leaders. Highly qualified investigators are available, and there are many Western-trained with excellent English language skills, which smoothens communications for international trials. Alongside that, there are highly centralized healthcare systems and strong levels of governmental support, with a clear focus on attracting research (9, 12).

Arabic is spoken most commonly in the Middle East, and this supports a uniform systems language across the whole region. A similar harmonized approach has been put in place for regulatory requirements (12). These factors result in a region that can be approached in an efficiently consistent way.

Recouping benefits from ever greater efficiencies is, of course, a key driver for pharma companies. Studies show that trial costs in the countries of the GCC and MENA are 59 % of equivalent trials in the US (13), making the siting of trials in the Middle East eminently sensible, economically, with companies ever looking for new ways to reduce cost per patient. The high level of patient acceptance in joining trials also allows the acceleration of trial timelines, boosting productivity, and reducing the overall cost per patient.

As we have seen, there is currently a very low density of trials in the Middle East, which means there is a wide-open field for growth.

Global Trends in Research

Global Trends in Randomized Clinical Trials (RCTs)

Randomized Clinical Trials (RCTs) continue to be the gold standard for deliberating treatment efficacy and patient outcomes. Here, the most impactful trends for us to consider are the intertwined developments of increased digitalization of health data and the rise of the use of real-world data to produce synthetic cohorts and generate real-world evidence suitable to stand alongside clinical trial results – we will cover these two trends in the following sections.

Another key trend is the requirement to ensure clinical testing is done for populations which are under-represented in trials done in "traditional" countries in North America, Europe, and China (2). Jonca Bull, M.D., director of the US FDA's Office of Minority Health (OMH) explains: "There are biological differences in how people process drugs. For example, variations in genetic coding can make a cancer treatment more toxic in one ethnic group than it would be in another … Getting more data on these differences is essential for FDA to truly know that a medical product will truly work and be safe for all patients." (14)

Meanwhile, precision medicine is gaining momentum. Traditionally, pharmaceutical companies and treatment providers grouped patients into broad categories, not considering individuals. If you are a breast cancer patient, traditionally your treatment would be the same, within parameters (size, hormone-responsive or not, peripheral migration or not), as for any other breast cancer patient with the same metrics. This is changing with personalized health care and precision medicine, and with new technology developments such as companion diagnostics and other genetic technologies that enable improvements in an individual patient's diagnosis and definition of the best course of treatment.

Recent reports put the Precision Medicine market on a growth track to reach USD 65–75 billion by 2021, with an estimated average growth rate of 10–12 % (15). The clearest case for more personalized medicine comes in the treatment of cancers, where treatments are most effective when focusing on tumor genotype. But the advantages presented by precision medicine can also be seen in the treatment of rare diseases, where new next-generation sequencing techniques can play a pivotal role. There are an estimated 7,000 rare diseases, afflicting as many as 350 million people around the world, and of which 80 % involve a genetic component (16).

One area to expect progress is in moving clinical trial datapoints from electronic health records (EHRs) directly into trial electronic data capture (EDC) systems. The data entry and verification of trial data into the study eCRF (electronic case record form) is still mostly manual. Transcription works across all data sources but has significant limitations, especially human fallibility, which brings the need for validation and monitoring of the transcribed data. Source data validation (SDV) requires additional resource and effort. Today, sophisticated EHR systems based on common data standards and interfaces have become available; in theory, we can make the EHR-to-EDC data transfer a reality. This would give us 100 % accurate data while eliminating the need for transcription and associated SDV (17).

Greater digitalization of data has created a new form of consortium or collaborative research network among hospitals wherein the hospitals share healthcare data within the closed group for research purposes. Participation in such research collaborations with other hospitals not only increases the available patient data within the consortium, but also gains the parties complementary expertise by connecting with other researchers and principal investigators. In Switzerland, the benchmark for the authors is the Swiss Personalized Health Network (SPHN), a national and cantonal (state) effort between public university hospitals such as Universitätspital Zürich, CHUV (Geneva), Inselspital (Bern), and others, that enables the country to democratize access to clinical data between the university hospitals and enhance research and the collective expertise (18). This therefore offers benefits not just to epidemiology and outcomes studies, but also improves clinical trial recruitment success rates by expanding the pool of patients, remembering that 80 % of clinical trials are delayed, often for recruitment-related reasons (19).

COVID

Of course, one defining trend of recent times has been the worldwide outbreak of the SARS-CoV-2 virus, the virus that causes COVID-19. Disease knows no borders, nor time zones, and this new age of COVID-19 shows the great need for a global perspective to healthcare data for an understanding of disease incidence, treatment paradigms, and patient outcomes. To start developing a response in the battle against COVID-19, researchers and health authorities require immediate data with a global perspective on disease transmittance, cohorts, and success rates for treatment regimes, among many other indicators. Despite the expectation of worldwide vaccination within 2021, current outlooks are still for a requirement for precautions into the following years, with vast and continuing impact on clinical research, in research focus and funding, and in on-the-ground practices of running trials.

As a result of COVID-19, trial enrolment has dropped, massively. A Medidata analysis showed an average reduction in trial enrollment of around 65 %, comparing March 2019 and March 2020 (20). Clearly, the pandemic has posed obstacles to ongoing study conduct: lockdowns and social distancing impact compliance with visit schedules and assessments. Worse, trial facilities become inaccessible or unsafe, as hospitals are overloaded with COVID-19 patients. Efficacy and safety endpoints may be compromised, as COVID-19 results in excess deaths and complications throughout the study period. This can be detrimental, for example, in oncology studies, where survival is often a primary endpoint. Supply chain difficulties and availability and access to investigational products pose further challenges (21, 22).

As a result of the rapid spread of the pandemic, many disease cohort and treatment models are coming from real-world evidence, not randomized clinical trials.

Global Trends in Real-World Evidence

Real-world data (RWD) is data on observed patient outcomes, derived from sources such as electronic health records, patient surveys, clinical trials, insurance claims, billing activities, and product and disease registries. Real-world evidence (RWE) is dependent on RWD and, as defined by the FDA, is "clinical evidence regarding the usage and potential benefits or risks of a medical product derived from analysis of RWD."

RWD can be used to generate new prospective data for RWE studies, sentinel surveillance, postmarketing surveillance studies, market access activities, reimbursement decisions, screening for risk management or health-care system evaluation, among other traditional or innovative study designs. The results are the achievement of better-quality evaluations, representativeness of data, and external validity, while balancing costs and resource utilization.

In particular, within clinical research, RWD supports efficient trial design, feasibility studies, the identification and tracking of research cohorts and surrogate control arms and electronic Clinical Outcomes Assessments (eCOAs). To take an example, de-identified patient data collected across multiple healthcare organizations can be used for epidemiology studies to look at disease occurrences, treatment metrics, differences by hospital, region, and country as well as to identify differential treatment groups or cohorts by local procedures or medication.

Having robust RWE allows a quick response when searching for data on patient characteristics, or an analysis of treatment pathways to provide insights on disease incidence and transmittance, treatment success rates, and patient outcomes. RWE can support assessments of treatment patterns, costs, and outcomes of interventions; identify underserved therapeutic areas, treatment claims; and assess efficacy and safety of therapies in real-world use.

The value of RWE is in generating insights into a drug's impact on patient journeys and outcomes through the use of existing patient data. With enough good patient data, researchers may apply intelligent informatics methodologies to extract and interpret useful information. As the patient data may be sourced from many sources, locations, organizations, and data models (*inter alia* electronic health records), it does need to be rendered harmonized, or at least interoperable.

Use Cases – real-world data performance insights:

– Synthetic control arms: using longitudinal data to create virtual control groups helps reduce clinical trial enrolment, cost, and needless duplication of patient treatment groups for which treatment data already exist. Additionally, using electronic health records to develop and test synthetic cohort models is critical to epidemiology and disease progression modelling (23).

– Predictive modelling: data scientists can use EHR data to predict the incidence of new patients for a specific indication in the future. Those predictions could help in clinical trials to model incidence/prevalence of specific condition of interest for a site.

– Therapeutic insights: health researchers can show insights into frequency and volume of use of medications and procedures and changes therein over time. They can also monitor if new prescriptions decrease the usage of other medications/procedures.

– Healthcare market insights: create market segmentation reports, for example, monitoring the frequency and volume of prescriptions for medication across pharmaceutical companies.

– Compound-specific usage statistics:

  o "How many patients with the diagnosis X receive compound Y within Z weeks of diagnosis?"

  o "How did the number of treatments with compound Y change during the last two years and is it gradually replaced by a competitor?"

– Adverse effects/events reporting:

  o "What are the top-10 diagnoses within two months after administration of X or procedure Y?"

  o "What is the median time to re-admission after administration of X or procedure Y in comparison with Z?"

– Demographic treatment algorithms:

  o "What is the preferred (i.e., most prescribed) treatment for illness X in the age group 18–28?"

Trend toward Digitalization

The trend toward digitalization has come up in a few places, above. Healthcare data comes in all shapes and sizes just like the patients and patient population it is derived from. Data sources vary widely, for example, individual metrics such as heartbeat and pulse from a smart portable, or an individual EKG, or genetic sequence, to patient registries, or electronic health records, or claims data. Data can be structured, such as patient name, diagnosis codes, and medications; or unstructured, such as the contents of emails, audio recordings, and doctors' handwritten notes. The volume and diversity of digital data is exploding and, in healthcare, the number of electronic health records is growing exponentially as technology makes this information increasingly available.

One key trend in global clinical research is the transition of all healthcare information into digital format. Digitalization of hospitals brings many advances in patient care and drug development. As hospitals evolve by digitalizing patient electronic health records, they will gain advantages in supporting their research and clinical trials.

An electronic health record (EHR) is the systematized collection of patients' electronically stored health information in digital format. EHR systems are designed to store data accurately and to capture the statistics of a patient across time, thus relieving the need to share previous records with current and future caregivers. EHRs enable patient care to be more based on the entire healthcare network, instead of being based on individual care givers, thus allowing patients to be seen across their healthcare network and their conditions reviewed and treated by broader expertise, regardless of location.

EHRs contain patient demographic details, such as age and weight, as well as their medical history, including diagnoses, treatments, conditions, laboratory results, radiology images, and billing information. EHRs are often the best longitudinal record of a patient's journey, treatment, and diagnostic history.

The trend of digitalization normalizes the recording, storage, and analysis of patient health data. The importance of the availability and use of good, structured data is paramount for good outcomes throughout the patient journey in healthcare, but the advent of digitalization, which enables Big Data analytics techniques to be used on patient data, opens up a wider world of possibility in generating meaningful real-world evidence from multifarious data types and sources. With the increasingly high costs of developing new drugs – the development of a new drug could cost up to $13 billion – Prof. Dr. Carlos Kiffer, founder and researcher in infectious diseases at the GC-2 Lab, points out that "it is only possible to put together the pieces of the puzzle that make the process of developing a drug, better cost effective and safer for the patient, by using robust data and good practices" (24).

Healthcare is now delivered through a network of care-givers and services, a collaborative process between different healthcare services, both inpatient and outpatient care, different physician specialities, care centers, and testing services which are no longer exclusively managed through a single point of contact (traditionally, the family or primary care physician). Increasingly, with the advent of greater patient travel capability and telemedicine services into rural areas, it is not uncommon for patients to be seen in different care settings and in different contexts and as they search out different speciality care options. The article "The

New Healthcare, Digital by Design" (25) mentions numerous efforts between hospitals, within systems, and across systems, to be able to share patient data, from a healthcare perspective.

The power of these networks to improve patient care is immense. Not only can individual patients be cared for holistically through the entirety of their digital experience, but a better understanding of care metrics, care efficacy, and epidemiology can be derived by looking at care within and across different settings. Data integration is therefore critical to improving patient care and outcomes from the levels of their existing care, but standards of data integration, interoperability, data security, and standards for data anonymization from personal and private patient data are critical for success.

Remote patient monitoring, home care, and telehealth have been gaining momentum for some time, but COVID-19 is forcing through a (r)evolution in clinical trial execution, from recruitment to submission. COVID-19 research is hungry for immediate access to real-world data to gain insights. Digital health technologies that enable continuous, real-time data collection meet this need. Across COVID-19 clinical trials, social-distancing measures force widespread use of virtual connectivity, and remote monitoring and management. We are likely to see real acceleration in the uptake of new technologies and processes which can reduce the time, effort, and burden on investigators, clinical research centers, and participants (26).

As treatments become more individualized, patients expect an individualized experience and engagement with their treatment. Allowing the patient to create their own engagement has been shown to be extremely effective as in chronic disease management such as diabetes (27), addiction, and neurology (28).

Image data has also recently found interest in the pharma industry for clinical research. The goal is to use clinical images in the definition of patient cohorts during the preparation for clinical trials, understand disease aetiology, and anticipate the response to new molecules. For the latter point, clinical images additionally provide information about previous therapy administration schedules (begin date, end date, dose history, and combo therapies), TNM tumor classification status, and a baseline necessary in efficacy studies.

Privacy

As an additional concern, while there is more demand for data, there is greater sensitivity to patient privacy, security, and higher thresholds to ensure data compliance in the EU General Data Protection Regulation (GDPR), the US Health

Insurance Portability and Accountability Act (HIPAA), and the new CCPA (California Consumer Privacy Act) legislation.

According to GDPR Recital 156, "The processing of personal data for archiving purposes in the public interest, scientific, or historical research purposes or statistical purposes should be subject to appropriate safeguards for the rights and freedoms of the data subject pursuant to this Regulation. Those safeguards should ensure that technical and organizational measures are in place in order to ensure, in particular, the principle of data minimization. The processing of personal data for scientific purposes should also comply with other relevant legislation such as on clinical trials (29)."

With this in mind, "according to existing regulations on data privacy, when the identity of the patient is not revealed to third parties and the norms are followed, there is nothing blocking the use of technological tools to improve and accelerate the recruitment of patients for clinical trials," says Dr. Antônio João Nocchi Parera, a legal expert in Brazil (30).

The goal is "meaningful use," that is, that electronic exchange of health information should enable improvements in quality of care. The concept of meaningful use rests on five pillars of health outcomes policy priorities (31):

1. Improve quality, safety, and efficiency, and reduce health disparities
2. Engage patients and families in their health
3. Improve care coordination
4. Improve population and public health
5. Ensure adequate privacy and security protection for personal health information

Where RWE and Digitalization Overlap to Progress the Trends in RCTs

"Value for care" is now the mantra in healthcare: to be able to demonstrate treatment and therapeutic effectiveness. RWE from patient networks are critical to being able to trace a patient's treatment and outcomes and to examining the effectiveness of therapeutics in different settings and as part of different treatment regimens.

From an epidemiological standpoint, using Big Data analytics techniques to gather, make sense of, put into context, and draw useful conclusions from large swathes of EHRs can generate useful data for real-world evidence and disease transmission, as well as treatment pathways within a hospital's population.

While clinical trial evidence remains the gold standard for evaluation of treatment efficacy, there is increasing interest and potential for converting real-world data into real-world evidence that, through analysis and interpretation, can be used to inform healthcare decision-making (32). RWD offers advantages over randomized controlled trials that are particularly useful for research and can be applied to healthcare decision-making. They include the availability of timely data at reasonable cost, large sample sizes that enable analysis of subpopulations and less common effects, and the representativeness of real-world practice and behaviors outside a clinical trial setting. On the other hand, while RWE offers tremendous potential, it also presents very real risks, such as biases due to lack of randomization, data quality, and the potential for spurious results due to data mining.

The merger of digital healthcare and patient data networks has also increased partnership and synergy in a number of areas of patient care, but in clinical trials, especially between sponsors and CROs to better identify patients and accurately recruit patients specific to the clinical research and study design (33). As EHR data is the most accurate resource of clinical patient data, access to patient networks of EHR data is critical to clinical research.

With EHR-based patient recruitment, electronically sending a protocol in the form of a query to multiple sites enables trial sponsors to evaluate numbers of patients fitting a protocol's complex criteria across all linked sites, nearly instantaneously, and removing the subjective element from the process. With such a system, a trial's primary investigator starts a study with an exhaustive list of potential candidate patients who fit the trial protocol criteria to screen, cutting down search and recruitment time. Depending on how they are configured, electronic patient recruitment systems may screen for patients on a continuous basis and identify eligible patients in near real-time. This offers important advantages where trials are time sensitive, or for capturing eligible candidates directly when they enter an emergency room.

A report from an SMO operating in Brazil which has run recruitment for trials shows that the use of the EMR-data-driven solution allows trial staff to spend more time on patient outreach and screening and can find patients not otherwise findable through traditional methods (34).

Not only is EHR data critical for understanding where actual patients are, but also for effective study design and site selection. The anonymized data is also invaluable for retrospective studies, studying treatment regimens, and developing surrogate cohorts. EHR data is a highly accurate source for RWD to understand trends and care and differences geographically and within care centers (35).

Clinical Research in MENA and Turkey

Barriers to Clinical Research: Regulations

Strong governmental support notwithstanding, we do note hindrances arising from the regulatory landscape in the Middle East. Government authorities are now addressing historical issues, such as guidelines and procedures which are not up to international standards, but rather just administrative; an inadequacy of resources and coordination between authorities; and trials refused by one committee being approved by another with no change in submission.

Various sources define challenges still to be hurdled for clinical trials to take off in the region, standards, and practices for trials among them.

In their paper "Clinical trials in the Middle East and North Africa (MENA) Region: Grandstanding or Grandeur?" the authors outline a few challenges, including that of familiarity with local regulatory rules and processes, which may vary wildly between different countries in the region. They also mention the need for monitoring and oversight, following Good Clinical Practice (GCP) requirements. Informed consent is also raised, citing issues of language and understanding, among a local population which needs translation into Arabic, and a migrant population who might speak one of many other languages where translation may not be easy, or might even have marginal literacy. Lastly, in standards of medical teaching, while the region is home to many excellent medical schools and teaching hospitals, the authors worry that research design is not taught and scientific research itself is undervalued (13).

Quintiles (now IQVIA) quotes an EMA paper, which states: "There is growing concern both among regulators and in public debate about how well these trials are conducted from an ethical and scientific/organisational standpoint (including GCP compliance) and about the available framework for the supervision of these trials." (9)

We see a trend to shift regulatory responsibilities from Ministries of Health to independent authorities (for example, SFDA in Saudi Arabia, FDO in Iran). Meanwhile, site administration and registry applications are separate processes in many countries. Countries such as Lebanon do not require a Ministry of Health registry, or approval; site approval is sufficient to initiate a trial.

Compatibility, or harmonization, with international regulations is a mixed bag. Francophone countries are generally tied to French regulations. Turkey, meanwhile, has taken major steps toward harmonizing with EU legislation. The GCC has had a central committee since 1999 to oversee the setting up of a uniform set of regulations for the seven member countries: the Kingdom of Saudi Arabia, the United Arab Emirates, Kuwait, Qatar, Bahrain, Oman, and Yemen.

Barriers to Clinical Research: Patient Recruitment

The barriers to patient recruitment in the Middle East are a lack of awareness about clinical trials in patients, the complexity of study protocols, and social and cultural issues related to trial participation (36). Patients entering the process will have fears of being guinea pigs and have anxieties about the side-effects of the medication. They will have trust issues with physicians who may not offer effective services to patients during the trial.

Potential strategies to enhance subject recruitment, therefore, include:

- engaging a dedicated clinical research coordinator to manage the running of each trial,
- arranging for patient transport to trial site for study visits,
- designing a recruitment strategy prior to study initiation,
- interacting with the medical community in the local area regarding clinical trial recruitment,
- educating subjects on the clinical trial during routine outpatient department (OPD) visits,
- creating positive awareness about clinical trials among people through press and mass media,
- using technological tools to select sites with high numbers of qualifying patients and to identify potential patients,
- using technological tools to engage patients and to increase the retention rate,
- creating professional centers using a software-driven, full process management system, which allows the definition and measurement of key performance indicators.

Country Insights

As we have seen, countries in the Middle East each have their own disease profile. The UAE and Jordan, for example, have high prevalence of diabetes (the UAE has the second highest in the world) (13). Egypt has a high incidence of hepatitis C (12). Saudi Arabia has the fifth highest incidence in the world for obesity (6). Just under a third of Saudis are classified as overweight, just under a quarter are habitual smokers, and just under a fifth suffer from diabetes (37). Authorities in Saudi Arabia are aware of this and have given free health plans for everyone in the Kingdom, creating a model healthcare system (6, 37).

Country Insights: Turkey

Turkey has well-structured processes and systems in place for clinical trials and has had a long history in running them. In this way, it is seen as a model for countries such as Egypt and Saudi Arabia, who are trying to close the gap. The country's clinical research profile is developing, supported by new regulations that are in accordance with international standards and European directives. As a country with a population of nearly 80 million, with high genetic diversity, Turkey is a country that offers great, new opportunities for clinical trials.

The number of hospitals in Turkey shows an increasing trend. In 2012, the country had 62 university hospitals, 489 private hospitals, and 843 government hospitals. By 2016, these numbers had risen to 70 university hospitals, 560 private hospitals and 874 government hospitals (38). The number of researchers in the hospitals is increasing day by day, with Good Clinical Practice (GCP) training throughout the country, instigated at ministry level. Beyond all of these advantages, trial costs are comparatively low relative to European Union countries and the United States of America.

Turkey has started the regulation of personal data protection with the law number 6698 (KVKK-Personal Data Protection Law) enacted in March 2016 followed by the Regulation on Personal Health Data issued by Ministry of Health in 2019. Similar to GDPR, in the fifth section, Article 16 indicates that the personal health data anonymized by the data controller can be used for scientific purposes. Article 17 likewise indicates that personal health data can be processed for scientific purposes within the framework of technical and administrative measures, provided that they do not violate the privacy or personal rights of the concerned persons or constitute a crime (39).

Turkey: Challenges

In Turkey, the most important problem in the clinical research process is the lack of administrative integrity. Institutions act independently, budgets are unpredictable, and there are significant differences in administrative evaluation processes. The Ministry is continuing work on this issue.

Other restrictions that may impede site and patient enrolment include the fact that no payments can be made to assistant personnel (leading to low motivation on their part to enroll more patients than they have to), no advertising can be done to recruit patients for clinical trials, and no payments can be made to patients in return for their study participation (except Phase I). One further limiting factor is that investigators cannot be paid directly for their trial involvement; payments must be made to the circulating capital department of the relevant institutions. Researchers receive around 60 % of the trial-related payments.

But the major issues in clinical trial patient recruitment are the same issues felt elsewhere, around the world:

- Finding the right sites, with high potential, for trials.
- Reaching the targeted number of patients. To avoid this, trial principal investigators (PIs) give very low estimates. The numbers for recruitment in the country as a whole are very low.
- It is not possible to identify non-diagnosed rare disease patients.
- Hospitals do not have dedicated staff for trials. PIs have the initiative. This gives a lack of reputation among international studies. Only PIs with some degree of reputation are able to conduct trials. The rest of the researchers may have ambitions to run trials, but do not know how to get access to them.
- Currently, hospitals have no idea about their own numbers for ongoing studies, completed studies, recruited patients, budgets used/missed, patients dropped/completed.
- No transparency in trial revenues (cf. US Sunshine Act).

Solutions?

Ostensibly about research, conducting sponsored trials requires professionalism to thrive in a competitive world. This is valid for physicians, clinical trial centers, and even countries. Physicians should be GCP-certified. They should be encouraged to conduct trials. Universities should have programs related to clinical trials. Processes should be in line with international standards, and transparent.

Technology should be in place in every step of the process, starting from feasibility until the end of the study, to take advantage of the technological improvements and speed up the clinical trials management process, in addition to reducing human error rate.

Given Turkey's high rate of patient record digitization and excellent and consistent data quality, it would make sense to leverage hospital databases for checking trial feasibility and for patient identification during trial recruitment. Big-data-style analytics allow queries to be performed which can identify eligible patients fitting complex sets of inclusion and exclusion criteria. This means that even patients with conditions that have gone undiagnosed may still be found by triangulating on combinations of other diagnoses, lab values, demographic data, and so on. With a large enough database, patients with rare diseases may easily be found.

We would also suggest that centers should be built for clinical trials. The whole process workflow of a clinical trial at hospitals could be coordinated by these centers electronically. This would give transparency and efficiency. Clinical research centers have the potential to be a lightning rod to attract new studies to their local regional hospital cluster, by showcasing the clinical potential of their local population. PIs associated with these centers would also have a platform to present their clinical expertise and capabilities.

Conclusion

The countries of the Middle East have a unique profile which makes them an ideal ground for running sponsored, international clinical trials. An expansion within the region would bring benefits both to patients and physicians in the form of better access to new and advanced healthcare options, as well as to the pharmaceuticals industry seeking better, more cost-effective, high-quality clinical trials.

This chapter has been expanded and revised from the article "Regulations and Recruitment: Experiences in the Middle East," by B. Erdoğan, Ö. Şeker, L.V. Chin, published in the Journal for Clinical Studies, Volume 9, Issue 3, June 2017.

References

1. United Nations, Department of Economic and Social Affairs, Population Division. World Population Prospects: The 2019 Revision.
2. clinicaltrials.gov, accessed on January 26, 2021.
3. Outlook for Global Medicines Through 2021: Balancing Cost and Value Report, QuintilesIMS Institute, Oct 2016.
4. Middle East Pharma Markets Continue to Soar: Here's Why, Genpharm, 2017.
5. Iranian Registry of Trials (https://irct.ir/), accessed on January 27, 2021.
6. Cecilia Chui, Middle East: The new "promised land" for pharma? IHS Markit, 27 February 2015.
7. Carolyn Gauntlett, Diabetes in the Middle East and North Africa: A High Growth Pharmaceutical Market Receptive to Innovation, Pharmaphorum, September 23, 2013.
8. Charlotte Pineau, Charles Rink, White Paper: Pharmerging Markets. Picking a Pathway to Success, IMS Health, ©2013.
9. Vladimir Misik, White Paper: Expected Growth of Industry-Sponsored Clinical Trials in the Middle East Benchmarked on other Global Regions, Quintiles, 2012.
10. Farzaneh Roudi, Population Trends and Challenges in the Middle East and North Africa, Population Reference Bureau, October 2001.

11. Yadi Huang, Joao da Rocha Fernandes, Suvi Karuranga, Belma Malanda, Nam Han Cho, Poster: Diabetes Prevalence in Middle East and North Africa Region (Estimates for 2017 and 2045), International Diabetes Foundation Congress 2017.

12. White Paper: 3 Steps to Middle East Success, PAREXEL, 2014.

13. Satish Chandrasekhar Nair, Halah Ibrahim, David D. Celentano, Clinical Trials in the Middle East and North Africa (MENA) Region: Grandstanding or Grandeur?, *Contemporary Clinical Trials* 2013;36:704–710.

14. Clinical Trials Shed Light on Minority Health, FDA (www.fda.gov/ForConsumers/ConsumerUpdates/ucm349063.htm), April 26, 2013.

15. Precision Medicine Market Size By Technology (Big Data Analytics, Gene Sequencing, Drug Discovery, Bioinformatics, Companion Diagnostics), By Application (Oncology, CNS, Immunology, Respiratory), Industry Analysis Report, Regional Outlook (US, Canada, Germany, UK, France, Scandinavia, Italy, Japan, China, India, Singapore, Mexico, Brazil, South Africa, UAE, Qatar, Saudi Arabia), Application Potential, Price Trends, Competitive Market Share & Forecast, 2016 – 2023, Global Market Insights, July 2016.

16. Heather Gartman, What "Precision Medicine" Means for Rare Diseases, PharmExec.com, Mar 03, 2016.

17. Levaux H, Will the Impact of COVID-19 on Clinical Trials Fast-Track Digital Health Technology?, Clinical Pipe, June 19, 2018

18. Visit: sphn.ch.

19. Earls E, Clinical Trial Delays: America's Patient Recruitment Dilemma, 2012. Available at www.clinicaltrialsarena.com/features/featureclinical-trial-patient-recruitment/

20. Adams B, Global Clinical Trials Take a Major Hit from Pandemic, with Endocrine Targeted Tests Worst Hit, FierceBiotech, April 8, 2020, available at: www.fiercebiotech.com/biotech/worldwide-clinical-trials-take-a-major-hit-from-pandemic-endocrine-targeted-tests-worst-hit

21. Melhem F, The Global Impact of COVID-19 on Clinical Trials and the Way Forward, Technology Networks, April 20, 2020, available at: www.technologynetworks.com/drug-discovery/blog/the-global-impact-of-covid-19-on-clinical-trials-and-the-way-forward-333652

22. Global Data Healthcare, The Impact of the Covid-19 Pandemic on Clinical Trials, Clinical Trials Arena, March 20, 2020, available at: www.clinicaltrialsarena.com/comment/covid-19-pandemic-clinical-trials

23. Goldsack J, Synthetic Control Arms Can Save Time and Money in Clinical Trials, STAT, February 5, 2019. Available at www.statnews.com/2019/02/05/synthetic-control-arms-clinical-trials

24. Carlos Kiffer, The Role of Central Labs and the Importance of Structured Data in Clinical Research, Proceedings from "Accelerating Clinical Research in Brazil" seminar, May 15, 2017.

25. Douglas Drake, The New Healthcare, Digital by Design. *Journal for Clinical Studies*, July, 2020;12(1).48–51

26. Piekarz D, Will the Impact of COVID-19 on Clinical Trials Fast-Track Digital Health Technology?, HCP Live, April 21, 2020, available at: www.mdmag.com/medical-news/impact-covid-19-trials-fast-track-digital-tech

27. Dobson R, Carter K, Whittaker R, Diabetes Text-Message Self-Management Support Program (SMS4BG): A Pilot Study. *JMIR Mhealth Uhealth*, 2015 Jan–Mar;3(1):e32, available at www.ncbi.nlm.nih.gov/pmc/articles/PMC4390615

28. Visit www.peartherapeutics.com

29. EU General Data Protection Regulation, to be found here: https://gdpr-info.eu/recitals/no-156/

30. Antônio João Nocchi Parera, Panorama Jurídico da Pesquisa Clínica no Brasil e a Possibilidade de Utilização de Solução Tecnológica para Recrutamento de Pacientes, proceedings from "Accelerating Clinical Research in Brazil" seminar, May 15, 2017.

31. Visit www.cdc.gov/ehrmeaningfuluse/introduction.html

32. Real-World Evidence, ISPOR, available at: www.ispor.org/strategic-initiatives/real-world-evidence

33. Integrated Research Partnerships Build Momentum, 1 July, 2015, Centerwatch, available at www.centerwatch.com/articles/16403

34. Ian Rentsch, Keyla Deucher, Presentation: How EHR Driven Patient Recruitment Supports Patient Centricity, MAGI's Clinical Research Conference – 2019 West, October, 2019.

35. Research Operations for Secondary Use of Clinical Sites, EMR Fall 2019, Evidera White Paper.

36. Kadam RA, Borde SU, Madas SA, Salvi SS, and Limaye SS. Challenges in Recruitment and Retention of Clinical Trial Subjects. *Perspectives in Clinical Research*, 2016;7(3):137–143. http://doi.org/10.4103/2229-3485.184820

37. Pharma Sales Make Up More Than Half of the GCC Market and Are Growing, The World Folio, 2015.

38. TurkStat, Turkish Agency of Statistics—Hospital Number Report, June 2012 and 2016.

39. KİŞİSEL SAĞLIK VERİLERİ HAKKINDA YÖNETMELİK ("Regulatıon On Personal Health Data"), found at www.resmigazete.gov.tr/eskiler/2019/06/20190621-3.htm

Fatih Ozdener

Sponsoring Clinical Trials at MENA – Need for New Pharmacoeconomic Models

Clinical trials (CTs) are the most critical steps in pharmaceutical product development. The cost of clinical trials constitutes approximately two-thirds of all development costs. Currently, the majority of the clinical trials are conducted by developed countries and sponsored by the pharmaceutical industry, although there is a huge potential for conducting clinical trials in emerging countries (1). The economical convenience is among the reasons why numerous sponsors find emerging countries attractive in terms of conducting late phase CTs (2). However, the most important barrier in the face of conducting clinical trials in developing countries is compliance with International Conference on Harmonization-Good Clinical Practices (ICH-GCP) guidelines. The level of compliance with ICH-GCP guidelines in a particular country is directly proportional to the increased number of new clinical studies (3). In this regard, a few countries like China, South Korea, and Turkey were able to increase the number of clinical trials dramatically, and improve their ranking among countries that are conducting most of the clinical trials. However, many countries in different regions of the world are still struggling to overcome the barriers in conducting CTs. In the following sections, some of the financial barriers in increasing the number of CTs in Turkey will be discussed, and a new model to decrease the financial burden on sponsors will be proposed.

Financial Barriers to Conducting Clinical Trials in Emerging Countries

The sponsor of a clinical study is responsible for the entire financial burden of that study. In many western countries where clinical studies are conducted intensively, expenditures that are foreseen in the treatment of a disease, and those that remain within the standard routine are not included in the budget of the clinical study. However, in some countries including Turkey, the regulatory health authority requires that all expenditures of the clinical study, including the expenditures of routine standard practice, be paid by the sponsor of the study. Therefore, pharmaceutical industry companies with the greatest potential to sponsor clinical studies consider meeting standard expenses an extra burden, and do not make their investments at the desired level due to this additional cost. The average cost of a CT is in the millions range, and it increases in direct proportion to the phase of the study (4). Hence, the figures are generally too large to be provided by a single source.

It has been observed that the number of clinical studies has significantly increased in countries that have switched to a model where the financial burden of standard CT costs are shared with a sponsor. Poland is an excellent example in this regard, as it quickly adapted to sponsor-friendly budgeting guidelines and regulations. Poland contributed PLN 240 million to its economy from approximately 400–500 new CT registrations with this change only, and reached a market size of PLN 860 million in 2010 (5). In comparison, current CT regulations in some MENA countries including Turkey are urging sponsors to finance all costs of a clinical trial, whether those costs are standard costs, care costs, or costs that are additionally imposed because of the study protocol. As a result of this overly inclusive regulation, all investigational products, CT supplies, investigator costs, all laboratory and radiological study costs, in short, all expenses of a particular patient in a CT are being paid by the study sponsor. In fact, neither social security institutions nor the volunteering study subjects should pay any expense at all (6). These obligations, unfortunately, makes it difficult for sponsors to include some of the countries, including Turkey, in the MENA region in their feasibility studies for CTs.

A Convenient Pharmacoeconomic Model

In the previous section, it has been mentioned that the cost of implementing the necessary standards in clinical trials is an important barrier in realizing the full CT potential of the MENA region. Hence, new pharmacoeconomic models are needed in these countries in order to decrease these costs while not adversely affecting total clinical study investments by the sponsors. Understanding sponsors' burden better and alleviating that burden is critical for Turkey, and similar countries in the region, in order for these countries to realize their full clinical study potential. In fact, the benefits of a new pharmacoeconomic model would be too many to ignore, especially in countries like Turkey with feasible geographical location and treatment-naïve patients (7, 8).

Table 1 shows the breakdown of costs of a typical phase II clinical trial for the sponsor and the social security institution. The first case (current state) shows the burden of a clinical trial on the sponsor in a situation where the sponsor is burdened with all costs. Considering this scenario, it would be appropriate to examine the investments made by the sponsors and the government in previous studies, and strategize how to make a profit by switching to a different investment model through an example. In the case of Turkey, the initial presumption is that the average cost of a phase II clinical trial is TRY 2,860,000, and that the sponsor covers 100 % of this cost. Further, it is presumed that the true potential of Turkey is approaching the rates in the American and Western European countries. Hence, despite the fewer number of clinical trials that are conducted, Turkey has 20 times more clinical trial potential. This means that the standard treatment of the patients corresponding to the 19 studies (out of 20) that are not currently performed would be paid by the government. This implies that if the standard treatment of patients in one study is assumed to be 2 million TRY, then 38 million TRY would be spent out of the government budget for 19 studies. In this case, it means that the government would actually cover 93 % of the treatment costs and the sponsors would cover only 7 %. However, since the rate covered by the government is not *in* the clinical study, but *outside* the clinical study, it leads to the misconception that the cost that is accommodated by the government is actually low.

Table 1: Comparison of cost structure between the sponsor and the government, according to the current model

	Current State
	All Clinical Studies in Turkey (₺)
Cost per clinical study	2,860,000
The number of clinical trials in the current state	1
Unrealized number of clinical studies	19
Total cost for the sponsor	2,860,000
Standard costs for patients not included in one clinical study (paid by the government)	2,000,000
Cost for the government for unrealized 19 clinical studies (otherwise, it partly would have been covered by the sponsor)	38,000,000
Total Cost	40,860,000
Cost percentage covered by the sponsor	7 %
Cost percentage covered by the government	93 %

₺ Turkish Lira

Assuming that Turkey has realized 95 % of its potential in the scenario in Table 2, which is the proposed scenario, this would correspond to 19 studies, that is 95 % of the 20 clinical studies. Further, if it is assumed that the standard treatments in these 19 studies are met by the government, which is 2 million TRY multiplied by 19, a cost of 38 million would be imposed on the government. This means that the cost of the sponsor would decrease to 860,000 TRY per study, but the total cost of 19 studies would be 16,340,000 TRY. In that case, while the cost to the government does not change at all, the sponsor's investment will increase by 571.33 %, and the number of clinical studies will increase by 1,900 %. When the increase in the number of clinical trials for sponsors is divided by the investments made, an investment rate that is three times more attractive is obtained.

Table 2: Comparison of cost structure between the sponsor and the government, according to the current model

	Proposed State	**Proposed State**
	All Clinical Studies in Turkey (₺)	Expenditure Increment Rate
Cost per clinical study	2,860,000	0.00 %
The number of clinical trials in the current state	19	
Unrealized number of clinical studies	1	
Total cost for the sponsor	860,000 * 19 = 16,340,000	**571.33 %**
Standard costs for patients not included in one clinical study (paid by the government)	2,000,000	0.00 %
Cost for the government for unrealized 19 clinical studies (otherwise, it partly would have been covered by the sponsor)	38,000,000	0.00 %
Total Cost	57,200,000	28.57 %
Cost percentage covered by the sponsor	29 %	
Cost percentage covered by the government	71 %	

₺ Turkish Lira
* The assumption of standard care cost reduction in the case of a nutritional clinical trial in

Benefits of the Sponsor-Friendly Regulation

The current burden of "the standard of care budgeting" is a common restrictive factor for the expansion of clinical trials in the MENA region. It is proposed that if there were changes in the legislation, sponsors would be only responsible for the non-standard diagnostic and treatment costs of a patient in a clinical trial, making the clinical trial volume in the country realizable in a short time. In this regard, a 19-fold increase is proposed in the number of new CTs, and a 5.71-fold increase is proposed in sponsor costs following the acceptance of the globally approved model (Tables 1 and 2). Considering the huge potential of the MENA region, this increased realization of CTs will provide an opportunity for extensive participation by potential patients as well. This transition will not necessarily create a financial burden on social security or on private security sectors (Tables 1 and 2).

In conclusion, given the hypothetical strategic scenarios attributed to Turkey and other countries in the MENA region to reach their potential, it is advised that the sponsorship regulations are reformed, and thereby more feasible investment opportunities are created for clinical studies through sponsorships.

Acknowledgment: Authors would like to thank Dr.Jan Van Der Mooren and Dr. Ali Evrim Doğan for valuable discussions on this topic

References

1. Rajadhyaksha V. Conducting feasibilities in clinical trials: an investment to ensure a good study. Perspectives in clinical research. 2010;1(3):106–9.

2. Glickman SW, McHutchison JG, Peterson ED, Cairns CB, Harrington RA, Califf RM, et al. Ethical and scientific implications of the globalization of clinical research. The New England journal of medicine. 2009;360(8):816–23.

3. Ozdener F, Kirbiyik F, Dogan AE. Analysis of nutrition clinical studies involving children in the Middle East and globally. Future Science OA. 2018;4(9):FSO334.

4. Martinez J. Driving Drug Innovation and Market Access: Part 1-Clinical Trial Cost Breakdown 2016 [cited 2019 April]. Available from: https://www.centerpointclinicalservices.com/blog-posts/driving-drive-drug-innovation-and-market-access-part-1-clinical-trial-cost-breakdown/.

5. Mariusz I, Tomasz J, Jacek O, Bartosz W. Clinical Trials in Poland – Key Challenges. INFARMA: 2010.

6. Ergun Y. Klinik Araştırmalar: Türkiye'deki Güncel Mevzuatın Bir Özeti. KSU Medical Journal. 2017;12(1):50–72.

7.	Ilbars H, Kavakli K, Akan H, Koyuncu Irmak D. Clinical Trials Journey of Turkey-Long and Thin Road 2015. pp. 1–5.

8.	Erdogan B, Seker O, Chin LV. Regulations and Recruitment: Experiences in the Middle East. Journal for clinical studies. 2017;9(3):30–34

9.	Zoltán K, János A, Miklós P, Csilla P, Zsuzsanna S, László N. Contribution of clinical trials to gross domestic product in Hungary. Croatian medical journal. 2014;55(5):446–51.

Fatih Özdener, Alihan Sürsal, Zülfiye Gül

Good Clinical Practice Training from the Perspective of Raising Clinical Trial Awareness

Good clinical practice (GCP) is the gold standard for the quality of clinical research conducted in humans, and investigator training is an essential part of complying with GCP. Some populated regions of the world such as the MENA region provide very good opportunities in terms of conducting clinical research; however, a lack of awareness of the GCP by the investigators can be a crucial limiting factor resulting in the under-utilization of this potential. There has been an absolute need in the MENA region to train physicians in GCP so that they could become clinical investigators. Moreover, GCP training is proven to be a very efficient platform to raise general awareness that motivates trained investigators to take part in clinical studies.

Types of GCP Trainings for CTs: Face-to-Face versus Online

The different learning modalities that are present for CT training are evolving at a speed directly proportional to the improvements in technology. In this respect, online learning (e-learning) is the way of presenting knowledge via Information and Communication Technology (ICT). Online learning is divided into two groups as synchronous learning and asynchronous learning. Synchronous learning is similar to the real-life learning due to the live interaction with the instructor, while in asynchronous learning, the learner and the instructor are not connected. Several instruments have been utilized for both types of learning such as the live virtual classrooms and webinars for synchronous learning, and the self-placed online learning and forums for asynchronous learning (1). In recent years, there has been a considerable increase in the number of both synchronous and asynchronous online learning programs for the GCP training. In fact, examples of such training have yielded successful results in Turkey. For instance, the Association of Clinical Research in Turkey has successfully launched asynchronous GCP training platforms (2). In addition, due to the COVID-19 restrictions, several academic and industry-sponsored synchronous training programs have also been started in Turkey recently.

Despite the effectiveness and the speed of e-learning, some interactions may necessitate face-to-face communication in order to achieve learning in depth.

E-learning, especially synchronous e-learning, has been accepted as efficient as face-to-face learning for the delivery of theoretical information, and between the two methods, no evidence of superiority has been found in terms of transforming knowledge into clinical behavior (3, 4). The blended training modality, however, merge face-to-face practice with the web-based delivery of information and is widely used in clinical medical sciences (5, 6). Thus, CT training may require a blended training modality in order to facilitate the theoretical learning via web-based instruments while applying the necessary instructions via face-to-face learning.

GCP training has important contributions in terms of raising awareness and providing operational benefits in regions where the potential of clinical studies is not sufficiently utilized. Clinical studies can make a significant contribution to the health economy of a country, and provide an additional option for patients by providing innovative products in therapeutic areas, such as cancer treatment, where current treatments are insufficient. The general awareness of physicians is especially limited in developing countries and in countries where clinical studies are neglected. However, a number of physicians participating in research have partial awareness on this matter.

In the case that a standard GCP training is intended to raise such awareness, the most effective strategy to follow is to involve different stakeholders of the clinical studies in the training program. In line with this strategy, it is important that not only formal knowledge is shared in their field, but also an operational experience is provided through the training.

Role of Regulatory Authority

In addition to arranging clinical research operations in a country, the regulatory authority has the role and responsibility of organizing clinical research training by issuing regulations and guidelines. Following the regulations published in the field of clinical studies in Turkey, "Guidance on educational programming and evaluation principles in clinical research" was published. This guideline plays an important role in the arena of clinical trials in terms of the accreditation of the GCP training. Moreover, the guide has provided a standard for GCP training in terms of basic principles, practice, evaluation, trainers, and requirements.

According to the guidance, fundamental principles for GCP training are summarized as follows (7):

- The number of participants in face-to-face training should range between 20 and 80 for optimum interaction during the training.

- Training should include a minimum of two separate workshops related to the subject.
- Training should be performed in an environment with adequate electronic equipment and an area suitable for the seating arrangement.
- It must be mandatory to have an experienced course coordinator who can answer administrative and educational questions asked by participants.
- During the whole training, a quality assurance officer should evaluate the presentations, and the capacity of the instructors and their interest toward the participants.
- Duration of presentations and workshops should not exceed 45 minutes and 3 hours, respectively, and all registered instructors should be present during training.
- Expectations of participants should be questioned and evaluated prior to the training.
- In order to test the levels of knowledge of the participants before training, a test composed of a minimum of 10 questions should be administered.
- Attendance should be recorded during every presentation.
- Summary of the previous instruction should be made in the case of lectures lasting more than one day. Prior to the advanced training followed by basic training, a brief summary should be presented to the participants in order to test their knowledge and evaluate their qualifications for advanced training.

An Example: GCP Trainings Conducted in Turkey

Considering the abovementioned guideline published by the Ministry of Health, a series of GCP trainings were started in Turkey by different independent groups in an effort to increase the number of potential investigators, and increase the general awareness among physicians in the country. Where possible, the trainings were performed so that different stakeholders in clinical research could be represented in the agenda with their specific topics of expertise. The trainings were accredited by the Clinical Trials Department of the Ministry of Health, and the investigators who completed the training successfully were certified to run clinical research in the country and/or to become an ethics committee member in various institutions. Table 1 below summarizes exemplary topics and instructor profiles that can exert the highest impact in an exemplary "Introduction to clinical research/basic training course" program, in which clinical researchers participate the most. It has been suggested, through the feedbacks from both educators and participants in the trainings carried out in recent years, that the position and the experience of the instructor plays a critical role both in the quality of the education and in raising awareness. The majority of the feedbacks was obtained for each school via a questionnaire containing a scale and an open-ended feedback section. These feedbacks were later reported to the Ministry of Health with a summary of the outcome, and the list of participants that were awarded with certificates. These schools where the training evaluations took place received great interest from physicians, and there has been a huge demand for the establishment of future schools. In fact, there has already been quite a number of participant investigators, who approached sponsors for the possibility of inclusion in clinical trials.

Table 1: Examples of instructor profiles and training programs that attracted the most participation

Introductory meeting to Good Clinical Practices Training	Course coordinator
Pre-training evaluation	All participants
Good Clinical Practice (GCP) and Helsinki	President of the Clinical Studies Association
Voluntary Informed Consent (VIF)	An experienced clinical research physician
(VIF) Workshop	All participants
Responsibilities of the parties: Researcher	An experienced clinical research physician
Responsibilities of the parties: Duties and responsibilities of the ethical committees	Chairman of the ethics committee
Responsibilities of the parties: Regulatory authority	An authorized clinical study in the regulatory authority
Responsibilities of the parties: Sponsor	Preferably an official of the product development department in the industry
Adverse event declarations	An official from the regulatory authority pharmacovigilance department
Workshop (responsibilities of the parties)	All participants
Investigator initiated studies	An experienced sponsor researcher or a sponsor official
Epidemiological/observational studies and clinical trials with drugs	An experienced clinical research physician
Quality management and monitoring	An experienced quality assurance officer from the industry

It is concluded that running GCP training programs is of great importance in raising awareness about clinical research and increasing the investigator potential, that is readily available in the country, for the inclusion into global and local clinical trials. The publication of guidelines for GCP trainings by the regulatory authority is of critical importance in particular. Guides such as the one mentioned in this section both ensure the quality of education and provide a platform to monitor the development of the potential in countries that undergo these trainings.

References

1. What Are Synchronous and Asynchronous eLearning? CommLab India, Rapid eLearning Solutions, Online Training, 2019 [cited 2019 December, 2019]. Available from: https://blog.commlabindia.com/elearning-design/types-of-elearning.

2. Association CR. Clinical Research Association Distance Education Programs 2018 [cited 2021 May]. Available from: http://www.kaduzem.org.

3. Aggarwal R, Gupte N, Kass N, Taylor H, Ali J, Bhan A, et al. A comparison of online versus on-site training in health research methodology: a randomized study. BMC medical education. 2011;11:37, 1–10

4. Lawn S, Zhi X, Morello A. An integrative review of e-learning in the delivery of self-management support training for health professionals. BMC medical education. 2017;17(1):183, 1–16

5. Banihashem SK, Rezaei E, Badali M, Dana A. The Impact of Using Blended Learning on Students' Creativity. Innovation and creativity in human science. 2014; 4:1, 113–127

6. Makhdoom N, Khoshhal KI, Algaidi S, Heissam K, Zolaly MA. 'Blended learning' as an effective teaching and learning strategy in clinical medicine: a comparative cross-sectional university-based study. Journal of Taibah University Medical Sciences. 2013;8(1):12–7.

7. T. C. Ministry of Health TPaMDA. Basic Legislation on Clinical Trials2016 May, 2016. 388 p.